FIND WHERE THE WIND GOES

MOMENTS FROM MY LIFE

. . .

DR. MAE JEMISON

SCHOLASTIC INC.

New York Toronto London Auckland Sydney
Mexico City New Delhi Hong Kong Buenos Aires

No part of this publication may be reproduced in whole or in part, or stored in a retrieval system, or transmitted in any form or by any means, electronic, mechanical, photocopying, recording, or otherwise, without written permission of the publisher. For information regarding permission, write to Scholastic Inc., Attention: Permissions Department, 557 Broadway, New York, NY 10012.

ISBN 0-439-13196-0

12 11 10 9 8 7 6 5 4 3   4 5 6 7 8/ 0

Printed in the U.S.A   23

First Scholastic Trade paperback printing, January 2003

The text type was set in 12-point Adobe Caslon.

Photo credits: NASA: PAGE VII AND INSERT PAGES 4, 5, 6; PHOTO COURTESY OF EBONY MAGAZINE, COPYRIGHT © 1992 JOHNSON PUBLISHING COMPANY: INSERT PAGE 7 (MAE JEMISON WITH NICHELLE NICHOLS); THE EVERETT COLLECTION: INSERT PAGE 7 (*STAR TREK*·CREW); ALL OTHER PHOTOS COURTESY OF THE AUTHOR.

DEDICATION

I wrote this book — really a collection of moments from my life growing up, not an autobiography — in response to a question I am frequently asked. What advice would you give to my teenage son or daughter who wants to . . . ? Firmly believing that example and experience are the best teachers, the advice I would give to a teenager is very much the same that I would give to a child or an adult. It is the same my mother gave to me. Pay attention to and learn from all the adventures you have in life, big and small, for within each there is valuable insight to help you throughout your life. Also, the lessons that happen when satisfying our curiosity, but which appear to conflict with maintaining our dignity, are particularly important. It seems to me that these curiosity–dignity conflicts reach a peak when we are teenagers (age wise) or adolescents in terms of our experience in a situation; we know quite a lot, but not enough to keep us from making the big mistakes.

Though focused on young adults, I wrote this for all of those who, like me, constantly have the answer to a life problem or lesson right at their fingertips. Yet while we manage only to grab and hold onto a fragment still we continue happily forward. I hope these stories and ideas are fun and enlightening for those young and old, boys and girls.

Here are moments when my curiosity seemed squarely at odds with my supposed dignity. So this book is dedicated to the friends in my life who with humor, always embodied the beautiful balance of dignified curiosity — Tiger, Pink, Gray, Pili, Mac, Lil' Mama, and Sneeze.

CONTENTS

This is me at Kennedy Space Center, two weeks before I was onboard the space shuttle *Endeavour* September 12, 1992, becoming the first woman of color in the world to travel into space. The earrings I am wearing, moon and stars, I got in Japan while training for my spaceflight. I got them the same evening I looked up into the Tokyo sky and saw an eclipse of the moon with Venus the evening star as its companion.

WIND CURRENTS:
WHO I INTENDED TO BE

"*What do you want to be when you grow up?*"

Looking around the room I saw the magical board with the colorful felt sun, flowers, and trees that stuck without glue and I thought, "I know the answer to that." I waved my hand excitedly, arm straight up in the air. I could barely hold my response inside while the teacher called on the other five and six year olds. They said *"fireman," "police officer," "mailman," "teacher," "mother."* I had my answer. It was none of these.

Finally the teacher called on me. Without hesitation, I answered emphatically, *"I want to be a scientist."*

The teacher looked puzzled and slightly taken aback. I can't say I know exactly what was wrong with my answer. Perhaps as my teacher looked around the kindergarten at McCosh Elementary School, 65th Street and Champlain Avenue in Woodlawn, inner-city Chicago, she was just surprised. Maybe she was thrown off by this skinny, brown-skinned girl, with short hair, who despite her baby-sitter's best efforts, might come to school a bit disheveled. Though obviously quite bright — this girl could already read and knew all her numbers — she refused to act like a little lady on the way to school with her older brother and sister or anywhere else. Maybe the teacher felt it was her job to help her students set realistic goals. In 1961, becoming a scientist was not in the realm of possibility for most people — and certainly not a little colored girl. (African Americans were still called and called ourselves "colored" back then.) So the teacher replied, *"Don't you mean a nurse?"*

To be honest, at that moment I did not worry about her thoughts. I was plain indignant. She doubted me, as if I didn't know what a scientist was or worse, that I was incapable of becoming one. I simply put my hands on my hips and said, "No, I mean a scientist."

Years later, after getting a degree in Chemical Engineering and while I was in medical school, I slipped and told a friend of a friend that I was going to apply to be an astronaut. He laughed loudly and said, *"You mean like the guys who go to the moon? Give me a break."*

Today, looking back at my life growing up and forward toward future possibilities, I'm struck by how the flow of life events is like the wind.

Events that change us and redirect our lives may begin very subtly, like as small changes in air temperature. There is a slight rustle of tree leaves; yet if one observes the accompanying signs, the next day's weather is forecast. The hint of a breeze that kisses your cheek may turn into a full-fledged hurricane that uproots trees and old ideas. Wind can flood the shoreline and change the course of rivers. A miniscule drop in atmospheric pressure may signal a tornado that in one intense minute knocks over buildings and blocks of the imagination. The next second the wind is gone, but your path in life is altered forever.

Life stretches in front of and behind us, made up of the actions we and others took. I wonder: "Is it possible to see the trends?" The small stirring of air as I waved my hand back and forth in kindergarten created only a slight breeze. What became of that breeze? What currents in my life began just then? What becomes of the wind?

My story, to date, is not a mystery. You may even know the ending, up to a point. I say up to a point because I am still alive. My life, I imagine and hope, continues to hold secrets, new challenges, and good times.

I have had a career in the physical sciences and technology, but also in the social sciences. I got through elementary school; the riots in the Chicago ghettos in the 1960s; short natural hair combined with puberty (whew!); integrated high schools, and whether that cute football player liked me as much as I liked him; chemical engineering at Stanford University in California and medical school at Cornell University in New York City; Cambodian refugee camps, and whether my country loved me as much as I was supposed to love it; the reality of being a doctor in West Africa; adjusting to summers in Houston, Texas — well, just Texas period; astronaut training, military pilots, spaceflight; learning about death; relinquishing the dream to be a fashion designer, an architectural designer, and professional dancer; crushes on famous, fictional, and not-so-famous men; and quasicelebritydom. I went through all of that trying to find where the wind goes. And I am still not sure.

I can say however that I have learned that there are always hints along the way, childhood is filled with them; some I paid attention to, some I missed completely, and quite a few I just chose to ignore. This is a brief collection of some moments from my life — large, small, and medium-sized moments that taught me lessons and carried me aloft to this place, this day. I want to share these with you now, for they were some of my best clues. I know there will definitely be more to come — 'cause the wind never stops blowing.

WHISPERS ON THE WIND

Daddy, Mother, and Other Folks

Mae Carol Jemison. I was born October 17, 1956, at Decatur General Hospital in Decatur, Alabama, the third child of Dorothy and Charlie Jemison. It must have been an auspicious day — why else would I have chosen it? As you can imagine, I do not remember much about that day. I am sure what I do remember is totally confused with what my parents said, and what my brother and sister brainwashed me to believe for their own sibling-inspired purposes. In truth, I am not sure that anything I recall before the age of two is more than a kind of "thought insertion."

I lived the first three and a half years of my life in Decatur, a small town in northern Alabama that had a population of approximately 30,000 when I first arrived. I remember hot, sunny streets and occasionally torrential rains. I had to look up at everything! Decatur was not busy — you could walk in the middle of the street in front of our house — yet it was quite adequate for my purposes back then. I just needed a nice, sunny, warm place near relatives to spend the first few years of my life. Since I have been back as an adult, I realize Decatur would probably be described as sleepy. Decatur is adjacent to Huntsville, Alabama, location of the Red Stone Arsenal, home to the patriot missiles used in the Desert Storm operation, and the Marshall Space Flight Center, where I would later spend many hours training as an astronaut.

The story goes that I was a pretty baby. All the nurses called me "Rosebud" because of the shape of my lips. I was told that I was a very happy infant who smiled easily and did not cry much. As I grew into a toddler, my father nicknamed me "Fattening Bug." I loved that name because I was thrilled to be growing bigger.

My mother Dorothy, my father Charlie, my brother and sister, Ricky and Ada Sue, and I lived in one side of a two-family duplex owned by my mother. Mr. John and Miss Ada, my mother's adoptive parents, were from Florence, Alabama, where my mother, an only child, grew up; it's also where my siblings were born. My paternal grandparents, Primus and Susie Jemison, lived in Talladega, Alabama, where my father and his older brother, my uncle Louis, grew up. Uncle Louis went to Talladega College, one of the oldest black universities in the country. My mother also went to Talladega College for a year. But they did not know each other and, no, that's not where she met my father. They met at a dance. I believe Cab Calloway, the famous bandleader who made zoot suits popular, was performing. At least that's where I arranged for them to meet.

When you're three years old, you really don't remember facial features. I believe you actually identify with the essence of a person's being; perhaps it is a smell, an electrical field or aura, the sound of someone's voice, someone's touch, but only the most obvious physical details are recorded.

I knew my mother; she was my mother. She was very smart, took care of me, and always kept me safe. As I grew up, I realized my mother was very pretty and what black people back then called a "tempting tan." I don't know exactly what that means, but it referred to skin color. My mother left college after two years to care for her ailing parents. For the first years of my life, she stayed at home, took care of us, worked occasional cleaning jobs, and sewed clothes to make extra money.

My father was tall, dark skinned, sometimes stern and sometimes playful. I looked forward to him coming home every evening. He worked as a roofer, which meant he was up on ladders and roofs handling hot tar. My father always wore a mustache, beard, goatee, or some type of facial hair. I found out later he was considered a very handsome man and his nickname was "Side Burns." We called him "Daddy" and we called my mother "Mother." Or as we pronounced it, "Mutha"—after all, we were in the South.

My most vivid memories in Decatur center around food. Specifically, "Bee-bops." Bee-bops, known as freeze cups in the North, were sweet drinks frozen in paper cups. The sugar that settled and froze on the bottom was the best part. The "Bee-bop Lady" (I have no idea what her real name was) lived a few houses up the street and sold candies and cookies as well. We walked down the hot, sun-drenched Alabama streets to her house. My bare feet burned on the hot concrete. But once I got the Bee-bops with my few pennies, the pavement would no longer burn. The syrup and water would condense on the cup and drip down my hand. My clothes were rapidly dirtied. At that point, the only thing that could make me happier would be to tag along with my older brother and sister on one of their fantastic adventures — or maybe eating a Moon Pie.

I am an adult now and I should try to be fair to Ada Sue and Ricky, my sister and brother, also known as the antagonists (and in truth, frequent allies) in various chapters of my life. Here are some facts about brothers and sisters. I do know that it is a drag to have a younger sibling like me stumbling along behind you, because your parents told you you had to take me along. Ha, ha! But that's life, and the price you have to pay for being older siblings. As the youngest child, you always desperately want to do whatever your older brother and sister do. You capitulate to all types of indignities, cheating, mistreatment, mind control, and physical restraint, just to be allowed to tag along. And your siblings know this.

So my very earliest memory was hard won. I turned

and looked at the backrest of the chair I had been sitting in. It was a light-colored, sky-blue, maybe satin brocade chair. I saw bloodstains where my head had been. I had just experienced a well-known childhood trauma: being accidentally hit on the head with a rock thrown by a sibling or friend.

Another early memory centers around what enticed my sibs to play with me voluntarily. Ricky and Ada Sue liked to blow on my belly and tickle me until I couldn't breathe. I'd laugh so hard I thought that my belly and sides would never stop cramping and hurting. They would sneak in and do this when my mother wasn't looking. I was also a welcome diversion during the vesicular stage of my chicken pox. That's when watery blisters, or vesicles as I later learned they were called in medical school, could be burst open and scabs pulled off. I know you may think "Yuck!" But, I have come to appreciate that "Yuck" is precisely the job of siblings. Younger or older, siblings are around to introduce us to icky things, to teach us humility, enable us to cope with the elements of surprise and fear, to present us with challenges, like how to get into their rooms, clothes, secrets or how to keep them out of ours. "Sibs" teach us the rewards of perseverance in competition: how to eat the fastest, to hold off from doing the chores the longest (my personal best for not washing dishes was two days, which included innovative hiding places); how to pass the blame and make accusations stick (I would always laugh), and how to get the best treatment from parents, aunts and uncles, and other adult members of the extended family. I could also count on Ricky and Ada Sue to support me whether things were good or not. We may have had personal skirmishes, but we always wanted the best for one another. We were proud of each other's accomplishments, and would help the others with tasks (as long as it wasn't washing the dishes!). The alliances between us changed as we grew — Ada Sue and Ricky versus Mae; Mae and Ada Sue versus Ricky; Ricky and Mae versus Ada Sue; or everyone for himself or herself — but we've always been very close.

My Life in Decatur: Learning the Ropes

When I was two and three years old, my day began with helping my mother get my six- and seven-year-old brother and sister ready for and off to school. I would walk with my mother to take Ada Sue and Ricky to Westlawn Elementary School. I always tried to maintain my balance along a curb that bordered a small pond. I imagined that small pond on my right had lily pads, frogs, and all sorts of other magical creatures in it. Later in the day, my mother and I might sew clothes, cook, or pay a nickel and take the bus downtown to go shopping. We would read stories together. I don't remember when I actually learned how to read. It seems I always knew my letters and sounds and numbers, and at least how to count to 100.

My absolute favorite thing to do was to go visit my aunt Hannah. She was really my great-great aunt. Everyone was so surprised by how well Aunt Hannah and I got along, since Aunt Hannah was not known to "suffer fools kindly." In fact, she was noted for having a bit of a temper and was not necessarily an "Oh, I just love children" kind of a woman. Yet, I remember sitting just as happily with her talking, solving the problems of the world, and learning. Everyone said that I was like Aunt Hannah. My mother would leave me there sometimes and I would cook with her. I am not quite sure where in Decatur she lived. We had to take the bus to get there or my father had to drive us in the car. Oh yeah, there's a story about the car.

My father had a Buick. He always drove Buicks. So I know it was a Buick I wrecked when at two years old I first stretched my "Let's explore" and "I can do that, too" wings.

My mother, my father, two of his friends, and I had gone shopping. My father pulled into the parking lot and my mother got out quickly to pick up some groceries. She found she needed help carrying the bags back so my father got out to help her. He left the car running, because he was only going to be a few minutes. It was the 1950s and gasoline prices and the environment were not issues yet.

Well, I decided I could drive and I jumped into the front seat. My father's friends didn't recognize what I had planned. By some stroke of kid luck, determination, and mimicry, I depressed the clutch, put the car in gear, gave it a little gas, and got the car moving before anyone knew anything. Everything was just dandy with the mechanics of the getting the car to move part. However, the steering part — you know, looking over the wheel, turning it to make the car go one way or the other — was difficult. The level of difficulty was evident three dented cars later.

My adventure ended abruptly. Daddy was incredulous that I had even gotten the car started and moving.

Mother was trying to figure out how I evaded two grown men and gotten behind the wheel in the first place. My parents were both thankful that nothing had happened to me. I thought I was pretty special and grinned broadly. I did not get a spanking or yelled at. My father's friends, they're another story.

All this happened in Decatur, Alabama, before I was four years old. I know because I celebrated my fourth birthday in Chicago on 61st Street and Ellis Avenue. There was caramel icing on a yellow cake with pink candles. Everyone was gathered around: Aunt Mary, Aunt Martha, Aunt Melvyn, Uncle Tootsie, my cousin Lenore, my brother and sister Ricky and Ada Sue, and my mother. My father was not.

Chicago Bound

We seemed to be standing in a dark cave. I don't remember if it was night or day. The warmth, humidity, and smell of diesel fuel was stifling. I had on a pretty little dress that I had not managed to dirty yet. Trains rolled into the station. The train we stood next to seemed to be alive as it hissed steam. It was so big! I was not even as tall as the wheels! I could see all the gears, nuts, and bolts; it looked so complicated. The train and the idea of traveling to some new place fascinated me, though no one else seemed excited. My mother, brother, sister, and I boarded a train in Decatur and went to Chicago, without my father.

I have very vague recollections of my mother not being completely happy and my parents having arguments. But what does that mean to a three year old if the disagreements are not violent or physical? I knew the husband and wife next door had fights. My mother and her friends did not understand why that woman stayed. Nothing like that happened at our house, so I did not know why my mother was unhappy. My sister tells me that my mother was unhappy with the job opportunities in Alabama. My mother had completed two years of college, but still could only find work cleaning white people's houses. She had left college to care for her ill parents, and once she was married and had three children, there was little opportunity to complete her college degree in Alabama.

In Chicago, though, my mother did complete college and then became a schoolteacher. She then went on to get her Master's degree and took up writing as well.

My father, however, hadn't wanted to leave Alabama. He made me smile. Just like any other three year old who was taken care of by her mother, I wanted to be with mine. But I didn't know why my father couldn't be there, too. There seemed to be a hole in everything.

Being little kids, once we arrived in Chicago, even under those circumstances, Ada Sue, Ricky, and I laughed and played, roughhoused really. We played tag, "Purple People Eater," and I fell off the bed onto the concrete floor of the basement apartment of my aunt Mary and uncle Tootsie's graystone. That's where my mother, brother, sister, and I lived. My head hit so hard I saw stars. I couldn't think. I couldn't breathe. I did not know if I would live. I was just there . . . and then I cried and cried and cried and "swup-swupped," you know that noise little kids make when they try to stop crying, try to take a deep breath, and try to keep mucus from running down their nose with the lip quivering, all at the same time? "Swup-swupping." I cried some more and then finally stopped "swup-swupping." Then it dawned on me, I was alive, still intact. Hey, I'm kinda resilient. My head was pretty hard after all. I could take a hard knock and still survive. The wind picked up speed.

Late that fall, just a bit after my fourth birthday, Ricky looked out the window and shouted, "There's Daddy!" My father had left Decatur and come to Chicago to be with us. We had only been separated a couple of months, but months seemed like a long time as a child. Now my father was here and we were happy. The family was all together. We soon moved from my uncle and aunt's into a dubious three-room apartment that we stayed in for only one or two months. We dubbed it "The Stink House," because the toilet common to the apartments on the first floor backed up too frequently for comfort. My father, not the landlord, would always fix it.

I started nursery school at that time because my mother worked. I was always so proud that my mother worked, because back then most women did not. I thought she was very special. The station wagon picked me up to carry me to The Growing Years Nursery School. It arrived each morning before my brother and sister left for school. I was dropped back home after they returned from school. I guess we were what folks now call "latchkey" children, because we went to school and came back without our parents being home.

During the early 1960s things were a bit different from today. Perhaps there were fewer real perils for children. But as kids we knew not to go outside when no adult was home. Rules which were not to be broken included not answering the door, not letting anyone else in the house whether we knew them or not, and not playing with fire. So at four, seven, and eight years old we did just fine for the two to three hours a day we were by ourselves.

One game we played was to peep out the door and look for my mother. She usually would arrive home between 4:30 p.m. and 5 p.m. During one of those peeping games I was hit in the head by the doorknob, and a "great big ol' hickey" immediately jumped on my forehead. I cried a bit, "swup-swupped," but, you know that passed quickly since I was already getting a well-deserved reputation for having a hard head.

Still Not Quite a Physician

I came face-to-face with the sorrow of death during our two-month-long stint in "The Stink House." There Peep-Peep, the Easter chick, met an untimely demise.

Practicing trampoline moves on the bed with wooden slats was not encouraged or even allowed, but, hey, it was fun. And let's just say that when I was jumping up and down on the mattress with the dear little chick, he did not jump out of the way with as much alacrity and skill as my four-year-old mind supposed he possessed. I noticed that he (I assumed that it was a he chick, but I did not know how to tell) was not making happy peep-peep sounds anymore after I stepped on him, and his head was lying limply to the side. I had accidentally broken Peep-Peep's neck. I was so scared. I felt so bad.

When I saw he was no longer jumping with me, I moved quickly and decisively. I cracked the window. I knew that people needed more air when they were faint — maybe this would work for other animals, too. I put Peep-Peep in the cool air to revive him. It was March in Chicago and cold. I cried and cried this time because I couldn't believe the chick was not going to wake up.

Ricky and Ada Sue came into the room, found me crying, saw the chick in the window, and started to call me a murderer. They called me silly because if Peep-Peep wasn't already dead, I was now freezing him to death. My mother took my hand, told my sibs to stop, and tried to soothe me. She said I was very smart because I thought about trying to get the chick some air. I began to feel better until my brother and sister began to reminisce about some ducks I supposedly helped along on their journey to the other side. I fed them too much cornbread when I was two years old in Alabama.

From all this, I learned that despite the darkness and hopeless feeling that often accompanies a cold wind, just hang in there. The breeze will warm eventually.

WIND CURRENTS:
THERE IS NOTHING TO BE
AFRAID OF EXCEPT FEAR ITSELF

Calculations In The Dark

Before I started kindergarten we moved to 65th Street and Drexel Avenue in the Woodlawn section on the South Side of Chicago. Our apartment occupied the first floor of a graystone building. There were four rooms in line from front to back: mother and daddy's room, the living room, our room, and the kitchen. Another family lived upstairs and the Hardwicks lived in the apartment in the front part of the basement.

Basements are mysterious, scary, and endlessly enticing and fascinating to little kids. They're filled with old paint cans, failed or postponed hobby projects, furnaces, coal storage bins, oil tanks, hot water heaters, and count-less boxes, castoffs, and cobwebs. Basements are inhab-ited by appliances that make noises and turn on and off by themselves.

The basement is always the epicenter of strange noises. *"It's the water pipes." "It's just the furnace." "The house is settling."* At least that's what your parents tell you is making the noise. Dark, dark corners and concrete spaces have a light dusting of cobwebs. Finished base-ments have sections that are all spiffy and nice, with paneling and tiled or carpeted floors. Some even have an apartment like the Hardwicks' in our building. Still, there is always a door that leads to a basement space that's dark or poorly lit. There are always doors to places where monsters or your siblings can hide. There are al-ways cobwebs and everybody knows cobwebs and dust are the signs of monster hangouts, places that can go dark in the blink of an eye.

I didn't like basements. I was afraid of the dark and basements scared me. That made our basement a very convenient place for my brother and sister to engage happily in their sibling duty to incite terror in the youngest. (Just a quick aside. The job of the youngest is to hang in there long enough for puberty and its hormones to work their magic. You grow so quickly that you catch up to your siblings in strength, stature, and possibly cunning overnight. Then, you can settle the score. There are a few other ways for younger siblings to teach older siblings lessons of humility even before then. More on that a little later!)

I was intelligent, precocious, tall for my age, nosy, and always ready to participate despite the dangers. Even if I was frightened, I was still "game" if it meant I could hang with the older kids. Let me amend that. I was IQ test smart, but maybe not too bright. I was always good for a laugh. Wait, wait, wait. I want to change that one more time. I was bright. But so were my brother and sister. And they were three and four years older than I. That meant they would always be bigger, stronger, and faster than me and could find new ways of fooling me. They were not old enough to feel that getting a few good laughs at my expense, blood pressure, and heart rate was morally and ethically wrong.

Back to basements. Now, the basement on Drexel Avenue was particularly diabolical. It ran the entire width and a third of the length of the building. In that 15-by-30-foot space was a furnace with a coal storage bin against the right wall. An old oil tank with a water heater lurked on the left. Snuggled into the front left corner was an old wringer-type washing machine. Towels, sheets, blouses, pants, and underwear hung to dry on clotheslines that crisscrossed the open space in the center. The door to the Hardwicks' apartment was all the way front on the left wall; hovering in the center of the rear wall was the solid wooden door leading to the crawl space underneath the house. It in turn was immediately adjacent to the outside storm door and the concrete stairs that led from the basement to the backyard. Altogether, it was a menacing tableau.

So why would a sane child ever venture there? Parents! There were tasks, chores, and missions to be accomplished requiring our presence in the basement. Getting to the Hardwicks' without going out the front door into bad weather meant one had to traverse this space. Mrs. Hardwick often looked after us, or we would play with her kids, Laurie, John L., and Paul. *"Go get the dry clothes and bring them upstairs,"* was a parental command that also meant a trip to the basement. *"Where's Tiger? Maybe the cat's in the basement,"* was another. To give me courage, my mother would always say things like *"There's nothing to be afraid of except fear itself." "There's nothing down there." "You can carry your own personal pro-*

tection, strength, with you." None of that really made any difference. Finally, *"Look, Mae, just go get the clothes,"* worked.

At times like these my analytical skills were tested. Should I chance the dangers of the dark and the deep alone, sans big brother and sister? Do I risk the possibility of disappearing unnoticed into oblivion and encountering the unknown bogeyman? Or do I travel with untrustworthy partners, who could keep the monsters at bay, but who would willingly sacrifice me to them temporarily for a few laughs if I let my guard down?

I chose the second, assuming I could use my strength, speed, and wits to anticipate when secret signals would flash between Ricky and Ada Sue. With luck I could beat them to the top of the stairs and into our apartment before they could slam the door shut, lock it, and turn off the basement lights leaving me alone on the stairs. I do not know the percentage of times that my strategy worked, but I remember the times when I was trapped in the basement, in the dark . . .

Suffice it to say that a good, strong, healthy six-year-old heart that restarts automatically was important to my being here to tell this tale today. How the rest of my organs functioned without blood I do not know. During the hour that my heart was stopped, I stood petrified on the stairs. My brain and the rest of my body continued to function. My mouth screamed. My eyes teared. I tried furiously to calculate whether it was possible to get to the bottom of the steps and turn on the light from the basement without the creature that lived in the coal bin reaching between the stairs and grabbing my leg. How could I evade the primordial forms under the oil tank that would slither out to grab me as I tippy-toed up to pull the light cord? My deliberations always led me to hope monsters didn't know how to climb stairs or that maybe they would stumble. Then Ada Sue or Ricky would open the door and almost fall on the floor laughing. My heart would start, along with the swup-swupping, and I would vow to be more on my guard next time.

I still don't like basements. But I learned they exist for good reasons. They are most common in the North because the foundation of a building needs to be below the depth where the ground will freeze in the winter. Basements are good for storage. Cats like to hide there. You can fix basements up and put exercise rooms in them. And besides being damp and dark, they're really not that scary. Get to know one during the light of day and look around. It's fun to understand all the pipes, vents, and electrical conduits that are housed in basements. Even the goblins are pretty cool.

I was a "scaredy-cat" as a little girl. And I am so amazed when folks call me brave these days. I always thought of myself as a chicken. I would try most things because I was curious. It wasn't that I had no fear, I just needed to know. My curiosity made me put trepidation aside and explore. Of course I always had a quick exit scoped out.

Keep Looking Forward and Smile!

I love movement and generally can hardly sit still. As a girl I would turn flips, jump up and down continuously, and put on a "dance show" at the family gatherings. I always knew how to do the latest popular dances. The "Four Corners," "Bugaloo," "Mashed Potato," "Popcorn," and "Skate." When I saw professional dancers like Lola Falana, Joey Heatherton, or Cyd Charisse dancing on television, I was mesmerized. Ada Sue took piano lessons. My mother signed Ricky up for accordion lessons (yep, you know: Lawrence Welk, polka) and karate lessons. Now it was my turn. I constantly begged to take dance classes. I would do anything to take them.

"Please, please, pleeeasse! I *really* want to do it."

Besides being very kinetic as a child, I was also known among the relatives as being clumsy. I stumbled and fell frequently, walking down the street, climbing or descending stairs. My shins were always host to a fine exhibition of wounds, scabs, and scars, fresh, middle-aged, and healed. I was a constant source of amusement to my siblings.

Once, when I was leaving the movie theater, I was talking and trying to keep up with Ada Sue and Ricky at the same time. I stumbled, fell, rolled, and skidded 20 feet downhill from the refreshment counter to the entrance of the Maryland Theater. A legend was born. *"From the candy stand to the ticket man,"* was a refrain sung over and over by my siblings to celebrate that particularly spectacular public tumble. In fact, they made up a whole song which still sends Ada Sue, now a child psychiatrist, into peals of laughter.

"Please, please, pleeeasse! I *really* want to do it!"

My mother thought that ballet and dance classes would teach me to be graceful and diminish my tendency to trip over things.

"Please, please, pleeeasse! I really want to do it."

Finally, it worked. When I was eight years old, my mother and I went to the Sadie Bruce Dance Academy on 54th Street and Calumet Avenue. I signed up for beginning ballet. I got little black ballet shoes, leotards, and tights. Excited isn't adequate. I was thrilled, enchanted, all smiles.

I took class at 10:30 every Saturday morning. I was entrusted to take the "el" train by myself. It was called the "el" because it was elevated off the ground, it didn't run underground like the subways in other cities like New York and London. I walked about four blocks from 65th Street and Drexel to 63rd Street and Cottage Grove Avenue, to get to the "el" station platform. Then I tiptoed up the stairs to the first level, keeping my eyes focused straight in front of me. I did not look down under any circumstances. I paid my fare and climbed the rest of the way up to the platform to the train tracks. I always stood as far from the street side of the platform as possible without getting too close to the edge where the train would come. I avoided looking down to avoid a glimpse of the street through the cracks between the wooden slats of the platform. Just that glimpse would have destroyed my self-induced illusion that I was not 20 feet above the street. This future astronaut was afraid of heights! I took the B train four stops to Garfield Boulevard and Wentworth Avenue. After I again carefully made my way down the platform to the street, I would breathe a sigh of relief. I had controlled my fear long enough to accomplish something I wanted: to learn to dance. I crossed busy Garfield Boulevard, 55th Street, and walked over to the house that hosted the dance school in the basement.

In class, we were first put through our paces with the assistant teacher in a small side room. Its silver painted walls always fascinated me, because the swirl of the brush strokes formed a pattern that criss-crossed the room. That's where we learned the basics of ballet: feet positions, arms, posture, and some of the dance steps. Then the whole class would go to the big studio, where Sadie Bruce herself would instruct the class.

Miss Bruce was always scary. She was a short, stocky woman, who looked strong as nails and never seemed to smile. And you could hear her screaming at the older kids. But, she always had something provocative to say about dance, something to make you think. She told us about Red Skelton. Skelton, a famous slapstick comedian with a weekly television show, made fun of ballet dancers. Miss Bruce made us understand that in order to mock dancers so effectively, Skelton himself had to have a keen understanding of ballet. Like I said, she made you think.

As dancers, Miss Bruce was tough on us: *"Don't clump around like a horse." "Land lightly on your feet." "No one wants to see you grunting and groaning, they want to see smiles." "Your dance should be effortless."*

Later, I learned that we were practicing for a dance recital. We took letters home to our parents stating how much our costumes would cost, when we would be measured for them, how much deposit was required, and most importantly how to order tickets for the recital.

My very first ballet recital! We wore pink toile tutus with satin bodices that had silver bric-a-brac across the straps and top. Small pink net flowers danced on the bodice attached in places. We also had to have pink ballet shoes. To save money, my mother and I spent the morning painting my black ballet shoes pink and hoping we didn't miss any spots.

Posters for "The Sadie Bruce Dance Revue" appeared

in public places all over the South Side of Chicago. The recital was held at the Chicago Opera House and it was huge — both the opera house and the recital. I never knew that there were so many students at the dance academy.

The afternoon of the performance Mother came backstage and put rouge and lipstick on me. She helped me get dressed. Then she left to go and sit in the audience. I don't remember really how the dance school instructors got us in place to go on stage, but I do remember seeing the bright lights, a huge stage, and what looked like endless darkness beyond. I knew Ada Sue, Ricky, Daddy, and Mother were out there, but I had no idea where. I concentrated on my steps. I didn't miss any and I remembered to look forward and smile.

The second year, following the recital, my mother decided to take me out of the Sadie Bruce Dance Academy, because she felt the emphasis was not on teaching the students how to be good dancers, but on the recital and putting as many bodies in the classes and on stage as possible. She enrolled me in modern dance classes with Michelle Madison at the Jane Addams Hull House Association Community Center on 67th Street and Eberhardt Avenue. I already was taking ceramics and art classes there.

Mrs. Madison was a beautiful young black woman in her early twenties, who looked like my vision of a dancer. She came to class with her leotards and tights under a long wrap skirt, or a short miniskirt. She wore a stylish warm coat and boots. She was conscious of her body and her carriage in a very unselfconscious manner. She had muscular arms, back, and torso but was lithe, liquid, and smooth. She was strong, but delicacy of movement was there. She sweated. In a word her body exuded confidence. It was neither timid nor afraid.

Every Saturday morning Mrs. Madison would work us very hard with basic dance movements, techniques, and exercises. There I learned precisely what a contraction, arch, flat back, point, flex, and plié should look like. We did pike situps, held relevés, and worked on our "turn-outs." Then, we would learn complicated dance routines that always challenged me to understand shape, form, and rhythm. Mrs. Madison would correct my movements and make me hold them. I grew stronger with her. I gained an appreciation for hard work, physical strength, and grace that has stayed with me through the years. Lola Falana, watch out!

SIROCCO:
A HOT, INTENSE WIND

Stoop sitting was a major pastime for kids in Chicago in the summer. A stoop was any place outside of the house that was big enough for more than one body to occupy. A stoop could support a small congregation. A stoop needed to be close to the sidewalk. The perfect stoop was a small porch that led directly to the sidewalk or a doorway with a small step for a landing on the apartment buildings. Congregations often centered on the concrete stairs leading up to the entrances to the graystone buildings. It seemed that at times everybody and his brother would be sitting out on the stoop when you needed to pass. The gang members particularly seemed to like stoops.

I really didn't have any qualms about walking past these stoop congregations when I was six, seven, eight, nine, or ten years old, until one day, coming back from my friend Jackie Brayboy's home on University Avenue, the lead stoop sitter in a bunch of stoop sitters called out to me. I was wearing my favorite outfit: little red shorts, a red-and-white checkered midriff blouse, and tennis shoes with red sweat socks. The stoop sitter asked how old I was. I replied ten. Then he asked if I had an older sister and did she look like me. I was afraid to lie. So I said yes. He told me to make sure I brought her down there with me the next time. They all smiled, laughed, and gave high fives. From then on I took a much more circuitous route to my friend Jackie's apartment. I became wary of walking in front of groups of guys on the stoop. My sister never went there with me. I told my mother. I don't think she told my father. He was someone who took action.

It was under much more serious circumstances that both my parents acted, changing our lives. The confrontation between my brother and members of the

Blackstone Rangers gang compelled us to move out of Woodlawn immediately. It all happened so quickly, early on a warm Chicago summer evening.

There were always stories of gang fights going around the neighborhood, and sadly, every so often, a tale of a boy being stabbed or shot with a zip gun. At Wadsworth Upper Grade Center (middle school), which my brother and sister attended, there was a story of one boy having his testicles cut. The images of the blood and pain filled my mind though I was still in grade school.

In our neighborhood, there were certain rules. If folks heard there was to be a gang fight, everyone would clear the street. At night occasionally one would hear a popping sound, possibly shots. Rule: Turn off the lights and hit the floor until everything was over for at least five to ten minutes. No, do not put your head up and try to peep out the window. The frequency of these stories and war drills gradually increased.

Drexel Avenue was very close to the border between the Blackstone Rangers and Disciples gangs' territories. These street gangs believed that everyone should be a member. They actively recruited any young man, especially if that youngster looked tough. If the teenage boy did not go along with their dumb behavior, someone was to teach the young man a violent lesson. Young men had to choose sides.

My brother Ricky had grown quickly. By the time he was twelve years old, his nickname was "Bear" because he was muscular, dark-skinned, and quite handsome. At Wadsworth everyone thought he was older. He was chosen to attend the Early Involvement Program at Hyde Park High School to learn to play the bass fiddle. He was accosted regularly by the Blackstone Rangers as he walked or rode the bus back and forth.

By the time he was fourteen, Ricky had grown to look considerably older. He went to Lindblom Technical High School, a magnet school outside of our district. So none of the gang members around our neighborhood knew him as a cohort. Besides, my mother and father would not have tolerated Ricky being in a gang in any form or fashion. Period. But my daddy didn't raise no punk, so this particular afternoon was bound to happen.

Our usual circle of friends, Ada Sue, Ricky and I, the Allen kids from next door, and the Mitchells from across the alley, were sitting out on the front porch of our building and the Allens' house. Yeah, we were stoop sitting. Talking, jumping Double Dutch, playing tag, playing teenagers being cool. Ada Sue, Zandra, Sheldon,

Artie, Roxanne, and Ricky were all in high school. Debbie, Stanley, Joe Joe, and I were preteens, just getting ready to start middle school. Debbie and I were on the sidewalk jumping rope or playing hopscotch. My brother, Artie, and Sheldon were sitting on the stoop of the Allens' house. Stanley was sitting on our porch. Just a lazy spring afternoon on Drexel Avenue until about six older teenage boys eased down the street. One openly carried a chain. Another toted a pipe.

Everyone paused as these teenagers approached. They stopped in front of the Allens' house and said something to Ricky. He stood up. Words started to pass. I don't remember all the comments, but I do remember standing, not saying anything. Maybe my feet were stuck. We waited to see what would happen, all eyes were riveted to the confrontation.

Danger doesn't register with some people; with others it does. The conversation between my brother and these hoodlums, one with a chain, another with a lead pipe, became more heated. Everyone started to get nervous, afraid. How would I help? It couldn't really be serious, could it?

I jumped at the noise behind me. Our front door flew open and a booming woman's voice commanded, "*What the hell is going on out here?"* There was my mother standing in the door with a pistol, very serious. Everyone's mouths dropped open.

One of the hoodlums immediately said, "Nothing, nothing." The leader attempted to find his bravado and said, "We were just talking."

Mrs. Dorothy Jemison, schoolteacher at Beethoven Elementary School in the Robert Taylor Homes projects by day, mother of a fourteen-year-old black boy growing up in the inner city of Chicago at all times, brooked no back talk. She merely stated, "Get the hell away from my son and this house. Don't let me see you little hoodlums around here again. Don't ever talk to my son again or you will have to deal with me and his daddy." In an effort to salvage a bit of dignity, the teenagers tried to "pimp" off — that is, they strutted with a slight limp as if one leg were slightly shorter than the other. They walked slowly, but they left.

Everyone began to talk excitedly. How did our mother find out? She had been in the kitchen cooking. My mother told Ada Sue, Ricky, and me to come inside the apartment immediately. It was not for protection, it was for a conversation. Ada Sue and I had some very important questions to answer. My mother wanted to know why she had to be informed by Stanley that some gang members were confronting our brother? It seems while everyone else was watching the show, Stanley who was one of those "fraidy-cat" kids, but actually quite smart, had the wherewithal and sense to notice a dangerous situation and slip into our apartment. He shouted, "Mrs. Jemison, there are some Blackstone Rangers out there trying to beat up Ricky."

My mother wanted us to understand that her signal to action should have been from my sister or me. We should not have been gawking. This had been a very dangerous and volatile situation, we should have informed her. We already knew that if one of us ever got into a fight we were expected, no, required to help out. It didn't matter how big the other kids were. But we were also expected to use good judgement and get someone who could help. My sister and I were punished for lack of action in this incident.

My mother called my father at work and told him what had happened. Daddy came straight home. Daddy, Mother, and Ricky got into the car and drove around the neighborhood looking for the gang members. My father wanted to reinforce my mother's message. Unbeknownst to me, once my father had followed my brother on the way to the Hyde Park High School Early Involvement Program when he was in seventh grade. My parents wanted to understand why Ricky was having attendance problems and poor grades. My father saw his twelve-year-old son harassed by two high school students on the way to better his education. Though my father believed in his son learning to fight his own battles, he also took care of his family. So Charlie Jemison, aka "Sideburns," got out of his car, collared these teenagers and let them know in no uncertain terms that they were never, ever to bother this particular boy. Ever.

After that, my mother was absolutely adamant that we move from Woodlawn. The rapidity with which she made arrangements is only clear to me now. That September, before I had attended Wadsworth Upper Grade Center for more than three weeks, we left 65th Street and Drexel Avenue where I had lived for seven years and moved into Morgan Park at 112th Street near Vincennes. We moved from the all-black ghetto as that area, Woodlawn, was beginning to be called, to become the first black family on a block in this far southside neighborhood. Though

Morgan Park High School and a couple of the elementary schools had historically been integrated, the residential areas were not.

In our new home, I could hear the sound of train horns in the night. There were rabbits in the backyard and trees and lawns everywhere. The street in front of our house was brick cobblestone. I sat in Esmond Elementary School next to blonde white girls who looked like some of the characters out of *The Brady Bunch* on television. No one at Esmond had ever seen a girl like me with a short natural hairdo up close.

At Esmond, the principal appeared to have a hard time understanding the note that accompanied my records from my homeroom teacher at Wadsworth. She said to put me into the eighth grade rather than the seventh, because my scores were all above senior level in high school. My former teacher had observed me and felt I had little to gain from seventh grade. The Esmond principal couldn't comprehend that, with me coming from the inner city. So he put me in the smart seventh grade class. When my homeroom teacher, Mr. Zaber, saw the note and my scores, he put me into his section of the eighth grade. He made sure I was challenged in math and science. The school had to put me into the smart eighth grade reading section.

As I rode my new bike through the unfamiliar streets and neighborhood of Morgan Park, I felt another wind swirl around me.

SOLAR WINDS

How and Why . . .

In first and second grades, I could not wait to do a science project. Ada Sue and Ricky had projects: an erupting volcano made with baking soda and vinegar; a working stoplight. I hung around my father and mother helping them to help my sibs. At times I thought I was more interested in the projects than Ada Sue and Ricky were, but it only seemed that way because I wanted one of my own so badly.

From third grade to sixth grade I had a science project called the Eras of Time. It was really a compilation of information about the formation and evolution of the universe. I don't know why I found this subject so compelling, I just did. And I still do.

I focused primarily on the evolution of life on planet Earth. In a series of clear plastic sweater boxes, I depicted a different geological era of time on the earth. You could call it a diorama. I went from the Azoic — nothing was really in that box because that's when the "Big Bang" supposedly occurred — to the Archeozoic, Paleozoic, Mesozoic, and ended with the Cenozoic, the era we are in right now. Every year, outside of class, I would research and learn more about the evolution of life on Earth and enhance my boxes. My Paleozoic Era was basically an aquarium with fish and plaster "fossils" I made for trilobites since I couldn't find any real ones. In the Mesozoic Era, the age of the dinosaurs of which the Jurassic period is a part, I tried to include plants that looked like what I imagined were plants of that time. To demonstrate teeth on early mammals, I had an opossum skull (a real one; its brain rattled around inside) that I retrieved from one of my dad's hunting trips. I used it because it was cool and the closest thing I could get to a fossil in Chicago.

I loved this Eras of Time project. To prepare for it I read about how Earth may have been formed out of nothingness. In fifth and sixth grade I discovered the experiments of Drs. Urey and Miller, scientists who, among others, tried to understand how life formed on Earth. They passed discharges of electricity through chambers containing what was thought to be the earth's atmosphere in its early years. They attempted to imitate early weather conditions. Simple amine compounds were formed. These amine compounds may have been the precursors of the amino acids that today form all our bodies' proteins. I read book after book on dinosaurs and evolution. I read how humans and other animals seem to have been in continuous evolution from one to another. I learned that as animals on this planet, we are much more related to one another than is immediately obvious. All these concepts were well within my ability to imagine and understand.

Well, maybe not. Understanding the beginning of the universe and nothingness is actually difficult. The size of infinity was tough to picture. I tried to imagine infinity, something that goes on forever, never ending. I tried to imagine nothingness — no energy, matter, light, dust particles — nothing.

Attempting to grasp and expand on these ideas was fascinating. One thought led to another. I couldn't stop thinking. What happens when I die? Is there nothing? What is consciousness? What is the essence of me? Does it cease completely when I die? At times I thought I held the answer, but if I focused too hard it would all soon dissipate. Philosophy, the essence of life, religion, and questions about the purpose of existence, are kin to these concepts. Answers we chase even in the wind.

Seeing Stars

I went to a camp in March during the sixth grade. The trip was sponsored by the public schools, to get inner-city children more involved with nature. To help us prepare for the experience, my teacher, Mrs. Miller, made sure we learned the constellations and studied local birds. At camp I remember looking at the constellations with her and drifting completely away. It was that sense of drifting away, yet belonging fully to the universe, that would take me to the library over and over to learn more about the stars.

Everyone in my family had library cards. Visits to the library were a constant part of my childhood in Wood-lawn and Morgan Park.

I would often walk up the hill to the public library, on Hoyne Avenue, about a mile away from my house. Sometimes I went with my sister, sometimes I went alone. Some of the books I could not take out because they were reference books. I would just sit and read them in the library. They had wonderful color pictures. It was at the library that I picked up my first science fiction book written for adults. I happened upon it while looking for astronomy books, which was what took me to the library most of the time. I was and remain absolutely fascinated by the stars, planets, and universe. I always wanted to know more about cosmology, physics, theories on how the universe was formed, and what stars were made of. I learned about most of this by reading on my own. Sometimes the material was difficult to understand. For example, learning that scientists knew stars were made primarily of hydrogen because of the spectrum of light they emitted was a concept difficult for me to grasp at first. But then I would take out chemistry books, study them on my own, and get the information I needed to become more comfortable with the subject.

I often stayed at the library until it closed at 9 p.m. Walking home at night, I looked at the stars. Though I was still afraid of the dark as a concept, walking outside at night, looking at the stars, was liberating and not frightening. Cold nights were the best because the stars appeared even more luminous. This, I learned from reading astronomy books, was because the cold air had fewer heat refraction waves. As I walked, I imagined myself working at the Palomar Observatory in Southern California, the largest mirror telescope in the world at the time.

I have come to believe that my fascination with the stars is because of their timelessness. Stars have always been a part of the world, the universe. I read that the star which appeared in biblical stories at the time of Christ was probably a supernova, and that it may have also been recorded by Chinese astronomers. I read that folks in the Southern Hemisphere see different stars than we do in the Northern Hemisphere, including the Southern Cross. While only logical, this difference spoke to the enormity of the universe and also to the many possibilities it holds.

I did not have a telescope as a child; I did not make one. I suppose I would have liked one, but, they were too expensive. Fortunately, I did have Chicago's Adler Planetarium. There I got to see the stars of the Southern Hemisphere and what the night sky looked like one thousand, two thousand, one million years ago during the time of dinosaurs.

Caught up in the vastness of the universe, I tried to imagine infinity as it existed before and after the "Big Bang." Supporting the "Big Bang" theory was the observation of "red shift" that told us the stars were moving away from us. The books said this "red shift" was akin to the Doppler effect for sound. The Doppler effect is what happens when trains move toward you and the pitch of the whistle tone is higher; then, when they move away from you the pitch of their whistle becomes lower. Then I read that Albert Einstein hypothesized that the universe was shaped like a saddle. "Now how did infinity get to be shaped like a saddle?" I wondered. I could not wait to take physics.

All that searching around for new books on astronomy, the beginning of the universe, galaxies, and stars with Greek mythological names brought me to Fred Hoyle. Hoyle, who was a British astronomer, wrote a novel called *A for Andromeda*. It was the name Andromeda, the galaxy closest to our own Milky Way galaxy, that caught my attention in the card catalogue.

In *A for Andromeda*, a radio telescope receives a signal that could not be a natural phenomenon. Its repetition and complexity has to be artificial. In the process of trying to decipher the signal, the astronomers discover that the signal is binary, that is made up of ones and zeros, like a computer program. They build a computer, program it with this Andromeda galaxy software, and watch what happens. The computer in turn builds a woman. As Sherlock Holmes says, "the game is afoot" — and I was hooked on science fiction. I read Hoyle's sequels, *Andromeda Breakthrough* and then found novels by other authors, like *Colossus: The Forbin Project*. Books by Isaac Asimov and Arthur C. Clarke became staples. I started ordering from the Science Fiction Book of the Month Club.

Why was I hooked? Inside of each science fiction book I saw the hope that humans would do better, that we could advance. Mystery and adversity challenged our character. I found imagination, fantasy, and possibilities between the pages. Interestingly, as a young black woman, I identified with grown white men who were the main characters and heroes. I identified with the desire to understand the world. I wanted to place myself squarely in the fray and compete with my intellect, skills, courage, foolhardiness, and daring. The mystery was as important and inescapable to me as it was to them. That mystery was unifying.

I was not blind to the fact that often women were portrayed as only supporting characters. They were not scientists or adventurers, and when they were, they were not the heroes. Their actions were not pivotal to saving the day. To tell the truth, this pissed me off. Not enough to stop reading, but enough to know that only one side of the story was being told. Rarely, if ever, was there an African, Indian, Chinese, Japanese, or Mexican character in the book. And if they did appear, they were never the scientists. Again, I knew better. There are sci-fi and adventure books that have women and people of color central. Authors like Octavia Butler, Marion Zimmer Bradley, Anne McCaffrey, and Madeline L'Engle.

Madeline L'Engle was probably the first science fiction author I read. In sixth grade I read the young adult novels *A Wrinkle in Time* and *The Arm of the Starfish*. They stand out as books that had women scientists and girl heroines. Those images were very important.

Years later, when I sat in the space shuttle waiting for launch, an incredible, huge grin came across my face. I grinned for that girl walking down Monterey Avenue on a cold Chicago winter evening, astronomy and adventure books tucked under her arm, neck bent back staring at the stars and a galaxy of signs.

CAUGHT IN THE EYE
OF A HURRICANE

"To thine ownself be true"

They say children ought not have to go through some things. But I think it's how your parents, guardians, and the adults around you help you to process the incidents that makes the difference. The outcome of an experience depends on what you have inside of you beforehand. In certain ways, experiencing some hardships are easier as a child, because you have more facility to heal. As long as the experience does not make you doubt your intrinsic self-worth, and if you have someone, an adult, to help you remember the importance of love and caring, you may even be the better for it.

Under those circumstances, certain disturbances can build you into a more resilient, responsible person. You begin to understand life from the view of the underdog, as well as the winner. You begin to differentiate the empty, harsh victory of the arrogant and privileged, from the sweet, sustaining confidence of doing right. And you begin to learn how to reconcile the difference between the philosophy of a system and its inherent worth, from those individuals who bend it to much less noble ends. You learn to commit yourself to doing better than that, even as the bile of indignation rises bitter in your throat; you rally against your well-founded fear and anger. But you must have the right circumstances. I was lucky. I chose my parents, teachers, relatives, and birth year well.

I Was Always Beautiful

My parents always discussed politics and social issues with us. After my mother saw Miriam Makeba, the South African singer, she felt compelled to celebrate our natural beauty. In the United States, nappy hair, especially short, nappy hair, was anathema to beauty. Makeba brought to the United States from apartheid-divided South Africa the Xhosa tradition of women wearing their hair short, to show the beautiful shape of their heads. For colored women, as "Black is beautiful" took hold, Makeba's hairdo was a statement. A political, cultural, and self-esteem statement my mother declared we would make. At eight years old I got my hair cut short and left nappy, in a natural hairdo. So did my sister. So did my mother.

Growing up I knew about Stokely Carmichael, H. Rap Brown, and *The Liberator* magazine. Malcolm X and Elijah Muhammad were common names. Around the kitchen table, discussion of Castro and the Bay of Pigs, the Soviet Union and communism versus capitalism, were *de rigueur*. We were forbidden to use the word "black" as an insult as was often the case during that time; instead, "black" became a word of pride. My uncle Louis philosophized on the words "Colored" and "Negro." What was so wrong about being black or African that we had to go to another language or euphemism to describe ourselves? Weren't white people a "color" too?

My brother, sister, and I learned early on about Black History as part of history, period. A black man invented the traffic light. Paul Robeson was an athlete, scholar, and unparalleled opera singer. Madame CJ Walker became a millionaire selling products for black folks' hair. There were Black Buffalo Soldiers, cowboys, and cavalry men. My father was part Choctaw Indian. African slaves often escaped and were aided by Native Americans, often becoming part of their tribes. Black people accepted all the hybrids and mixtures of people into their community, too. Society considered as black anyone who was part white, mostly white, a little black, part Chinese, or Indian, if they had black ancestors. But more importantly the black community accepted them. White people, too, who were considered outcasts due to marriage to a colored person or for other reasons, were also taken in.

I was taught about tolerance. Just because someone else acts like a jackass, is unfair, lies, or cheats does not mean you should adopt his or her behavior. In fact, it seemed that a cornerstone of strength and continued faith for many black people at the time was that they maintained the moral high ground in society. Uncle Louis and my mother particularly had frequent, long conversations about that. And how as a black person you better be twice as good as a white person to get anywhere. The proverb, "Two wrongs don't make a right" was well known in my home.

Helplessness, Frustration and Power

"Black Power!" When Stokely Carmichael chanted those words at a student rally in 1965, he meant economic empowerment, confidence, self-esteem, and independence. The riots of the time didn't stem from that phrase, Black Power, but from built-up frustration. Neither my parents nor anyone else I knew, participated in or believed that the riots that destroyed the black neighborhoods in cities across the nation during the summers in the 1960s were good. The riots did not directly help the black community. In fact, they destroyed many of the black businesses and single family homes. Yet in a sense, the riots brought national attention to the serious problems of race and equality.

In spring 1968, after two previous summers of riots, television programs around the nation were interrupted with the news that Martin Luther King, Jr. had been shot and killed in Memphis. My parents announced, "It's going to be *very hot* this summer."

That summer the riots and destruction came closer to our home. In previous summers, it was mainly the West Side of Chicago that fell into chaos. This time stores only a couple blocks from my home were broken into and looted; shops on 63rd Street were burned. Curfews were imposed. Daytime was no longer safe. We all stayed indoors.

In 1968 the Democratic National Convention took place in Chicago with the attendant demonstrations. Mayor Daley was determined to assert his control of the city.

Neighborhood streets were clear and empty even though it was the middle of the day. Complete stillness. The air was calm. There were no traffic sounds. A stray dog wandered across the vacant lot. Everything had that eerie feeling that comes with tornado warnings, but, instead of the pinkish, yellowish, hazy skies and humid air, the sky was blue, cloudless, and windless. It reminded me of the air-raid drills in school to prepare us in case of a nuclear attack by the Soviet Union. We would walk quickly to the bottom floor, huddle inside corridors two students deep, and lean against the walls with our arms over our heads. Then I would wonder if the world would really end in a flash of light and a mushroom cloud.

This time I wasn't in school and this was no drill. I was at home peeking out the back screen door, deeply afraid to look outside, but too mesmerized not to. My ten-year-old heart was beating rapidly, my throat was dry, but I had to see. I had run from the front picture window where I had a partial view of 65th Street, to the kitchen, where the vacant lot gave a clear view all the way over to Ingleside Avenue. I had to see.

And there they were: the National Guard, dispatched at the request of Mayor Daley. Walking, marching, purposefully in a single file line carrying rifles. They were dressed in fatigues, war costumes. They wore camouflage, combat boots, helmets, and held guns in front of them at the ready. Their orders were "shoot-to-kill."

My father was at work. Would he be safe on his way back home? The National Guardsmen did not seem to be there to protect *us*.

I was so scared. I was afraid the National Guard would see me. There were black National Guardsmen, too; I was also afraid of them. Children as young as thirteen had been shot and killed during the riots. I knew as a ten-year-old black girl that I was not precious to these adults. I believed they would kill me as readily as they would kill the Vietnamese we were at war with. It didn't matter that I was a United States citizen. It didn't matter that I was very smart, would probably grow up to be pretty like my mother, or that I was fun to talk to, and had unlimited potential. It didn't matter that I was a good girl and hadn't been suspended from school. It didn't matter because *I* didn't matter to them. These adults, these representatives, enforcers of the United States government would hold me in suspicion and probably shoot me if I was out on the street. So I cowered behind the back door screen to see who they were. They looked like regular folk — but ready for war.

I was baffled and I was angry. I made myself a promise that I wouldn't be frightened like that anymore. I reminded myself I was as much a part of this United States as the guardsmen or anyone else. I should expect as much from this country as they did. Goodness knows I was willing and determined to contribute, it was my right and responsibility. I can't just let folks blow up this planet. We as humans don't have that right. And we don't have the right to take other folks' lives and belongings, or to frighten them, as I was frightened then.

As I said, the good thing about being a child is resilience. Soon things settled down and we started going outside again. I forgot the fear and played in the vacant lot, ran errands for my parents up and down 65th Street, 63rd Street, and went to summer school. But I never forgot that feeling or the unspoken vow that I made in the summer of '68. It is vital to keep my humanity and my right to participate, but not to tread on others.

That unspoken vow has been so important in my life. As a civil servant, both as a Peace Corps physician and an astronaut, I had to take an oath to the United States. I could do this not only because I recognized the opportunities, but I also acknowledged my responsibility to work to help our country to fulfill its promise. Even though I am a person who at the beginning of this nation would not have been recognized as a full person — slaves were not counted and women had no right to vote — I realize that the failure, the wrong was in the individuals, and not the basic philosophy. I have the right and responsibility to expand that philosophy and work to make it manifest. We all do.

WIND CURRENTS:
AN EXTRA SPOONFUL
FOR GOOD MEASURE

I learned there are a number of indications that the world recognizes you as an individual, a full person, a human being with an identity. One is when folks ask your opinion and what you want. A stronger indication is when the opinion or what you want actually influences a decision. Another is when you have enough money to buy more than just your lunch at school.

One definite sign that you're an individual is when you get mail addressed to you, especially if it's from someone besides your grandmother. (Not that grandmother mail, great-aunt, and older cousin mail isn't wonderful, but, sometimes they write, you know, just to be nice or because they have to.)

Between the ages of ten and eleven I figured out how to get other mail. It was really very simple. I couldn't believe no one else had thought of it. You merely had to fill in and mail the free offers in magazines for Book of the Month, or Record of the Month, clubs, the ones that said, *"Nothing to buy. We will send you twelve books for 10 cents."* Cool! I didn't read that part where you had to commit to buy other things to get such a great deal. Anyway, once you start, the books and mail addressed to you never stops coming. I was the envy of my older brother and sister until Ricky noticed that half the mail was addressed to "Mr. Mac Jemison," because someone did not write her name in clearly. He got a good laugh out of that.

I got albums like *Mission Impossible* by Lalo Schriffin and *Hang 'Em High* by Hugo Montenegro. I joined the Science Fiction Book Club and the Science Book Club. I loved getting the mail. I didn't understand why I kept getting threatening letters for payment until later. That was in the fine print that a precocious ten year old ignores. The incredible thing was that I got mail from companies

I didn't even write to! That's how I received my first set of international recipe books. I don't even remember ordering them.

It was from these wonderful cookbooks that I tried many exciting recipes. I was already fairly good at cooking some dishes that I helped my mother with, none of which were desserts and sweets, because we ate very few growing up. Therefore, when I needed a recipe for a special cookie that was sure to be a hit at the school bake sales, I consulted my cookbooks.

Small problem. Sometimes, many times, in fact, I did not do a good job following the recipes. If I did not have the specific ingredient, I would substitute another I judged similar enough to pass. And I couldn't always be bothered getting real measuring spoons and cups. I would "eyeball" measurements. The result? Cookies that would never brown. Cookies that turned very hard. Cookies that sold only one or two out of four dozen. Cookies that taught humility. Cookies that said sometimes you have to learn to follow the rules.

UPDRAFT

Fall 1969. Miniskirts, platform shoes, Afro hairdos were starting to be accepted. Martin Luther King, Jr. and Bobby Kennedy had been killed the year before. Sit-ins and walkouts were common in colleges and schools across the country. "Soulful Strut" by The Young Holt Trio and "Loveland" by the 103rd Street Watts Rhythm Band were my favorite songs. The Temptations' "I Can't Get Next to You" was not far behind. The improbable dances the "Funky Chicken" and "Sophisticated Sissy" were the rage.

No other way to put it, my years in high school were tumultuous. I entered a twelve-year-old unknown freshman who quickly got on the wrong side of the vice-principal. I graduated a sixteen-year-old senior and student council president now firmly on the wrong side of the same vice-principal and perhaps a few other administrators as well. There were teachers who were very proud of me and I had gained friends and respect.

Since sixth grade I had been at least 5'6" and somewhat thin. I had worn a short natural Afro since fourth grade. Sometimes folks mistook me for a boy because girls didn't have haircuts like that back then. It got a little rough during puberty when despite budding mammary glands, well-meaning people in stores would call me "son."

You might think starting high school at twelve sounds intimidating. Was it? Well, yes and no. It was scary because these were high school students, like my brother and sister. I went to a different class each period. There were lockers. Eventually I would be able to try out for cheerleading and plays. I would take physics, chemistry, and biology. Many more possibilities and options were available.

It was cool that my brother and sister were at the same school. Ricky was particularly hip, and Ada Sue was president of the student council. I would get to do more strenuous physical sports and activities. I was already tall, so I didn't have to worry about being bullied because I was smaller than the other students.

Chicago has beautiful weather in September and early October. Crisp, clear days with autumn swirling in the air. I started school on such a day. My homeroom teacher, Mrs. Roberts, was very pleasant. She directed us to classrooms, the cafeteria, and gave us our schedules. Mrs. Roberts was probably in her early forties, well-groomed and fashionably, but conservatively dressed. She wore her brunette hair in a flip. She took a liking to me.

I had algebra, English, Russian, geography, art, study hall, lunch, and physical education. Believe it or not, my freshman year I got the worst grades and had the most difficult time in physical education. In fact, the first semester I got a "D"! How in the world do you get a "D" in girls' physical education in Chicago in 1969, especially, when you are very athletic, like to dance, and are good in science and math? I could do sit-ups, count, and knew the parts of the body; if not for the health class portion, I probably would have gotten an "F." How? Well, remember those cookies? You have to try hard and not follow instructions.

Here's how I did it. First, I didn't get my light blue, one-piece gym suit. When I finally got it, I did not sew my name on it quickly enough. I had a hard time polishing my gym shoes, keeping them nice and white with my name printed on the side. I was not really a slob, but just not as meticulous as Ms. Branecki, my teacher, desired. Then there was swimming.

My mother didn't want me to take swimming, because of allergies, but I really wanted to. I needed a physician's excuse to exclude me for the year. I procrastinated and got a bad mark because I didn't have parental permission to swim or a doctor's note not to. It all ended happily though. By January I persuaded my mother to change her mind. I started taking swimming and progressed rapidly to the deep end. By my junior year, one-and-a-half years later, after I learned to keep my gym clothes presentable, I was chosen as a swim leader and a gym leader!

My MO: Go for It

One thing I was consistent about was testing limits — mine and other people's, especially adults. I don't know if

I was actually aware of what I was doing, but that's what I did. My modus operandi, "MO," was to smile frequently and laugh whenever possible — including at myself. Life was fun. I imagined something I would like to do, particularly if I hadn't done it before. I would look around for an opportunity and find a potential way to get it done. I would figure out my best shot at accomplishing it. Then go for it. Yeah! The All City High School production of *West Side Story* was the perfect opportunity.

I Can't Sing, but I Sure Can Dance

I loved the musical *West Side Story*. *West Side Story* had a great plot, lots of great singing, incredibly cool dancing, and solid acting. Singing, dancing, and acting. I knew that I was good at the second, could probably do the third, but that first one, singing, was a problem. I never could sing. As a child, I had been famous for my off-key renditions of "Jingle Bells." I could threaten people with "Rudolph the Red-Nosed Reindeer." However, I had heard Ethel Merman and a couple of other Broadway stars sorta "sing-talk" their way through songs. I had great stage presence, a good strong voice, and wonderful projection. (I could make the folks in the back of the auditorium hear me!) And I could dance! My favorite character in *West Side Story* was Anita, played in the movie by Rita Moreno. So I decided to try out for the role of Anita. I pushed the limit with my "tongue planted firmly in cheek."

I found out what was needed to audition for the role of Anita. You had to learn the scene preceding the song "America" with the character Bernardo (George Chakiris in the movie). You had to sing "America" all the way through and be prepared to dance with the choreographer. Piece of cake. I can do this.

I pulled out my *West Side Story* album from my Record of the Month Club contraband, and listened over and over again to "America." I practiced with Anita. I learned to sing-talk the words with a great Puerto Rican accent (at least *I* thought it was a great accent). My dialogue was fabulous, again with Puerto Rican accent, and I could already dance. The day before auditions, I had my mother cornrow my hair. She still could not believe I had the nerve to try out for Anita — as I said, my singing voice was infamous. I was ready.

I sashayed into the audition hall exuding incredible confidence. The girls were paired with various boys trying out for Bernardo. They weeded people out quickly. I read lines again, several times with the best male lead. Then they had us dance. Piece of cake. I was good. Finally came the singing.

The director and music director sat together in the center of the auditorium. We were called on stage one at a time. After each person finished singing, each was told to sit in a certain section of the auditorium. As time went along it was pretty clear that the sections were equated with performance skill. My turn.

I exuded confidence. I had practiced this. I swished on stage. Anita was "attitude," if nothing else. I had my movements ready to go with the words. I sang. I swished. I smiled and swished. And I was told to leave the stage and go sit behind the director. I didn't move. I asked again. "Behind the director?" I couldn't believe it.

When I got home my mother asked me how things went in her soft "motherly concern" voice. I told her I got called back for next Saturday and they had placed me in the section with just five other girls. The girls who could *really* sing. My mother just shook her head. I had made it. Vindicated!

I worked even harder over the following week to be ready for the callback. About ten girls were called back, including me. Since the show ran longer than a week, the directors were going to choose two to play Anita. All things being equal, I had a one in five chance, better odds than before.

Saturday morning. Hair freshly cornrowed, little bit of makeup, cheerful bright-colored clothes, leotards and hip-hugging bell bottom pants, plenty of smiles and attitude.

This time auditions did not take place in an auditorium, but rather in the dance studio of the high school downtown. We danced. I did very well. We dialogued. Cool! Still looking good. Then they sent some of us over to the piano with the music director. We had to learn a new song. Now, I know exactly what you are thinking: "busted!" But, I was still cool and confident because I was prepared. I had learned all of Anita's songs. I was ready to sing-talk my way to the part. I had contingency plans. I was not a Girl Scout, but I came prepared.

The music director pulled out the music and played "Maria" or . . . I don't even remember. It wasn't any song that Anita ever remotely sang. The jig was up. I just smiled, tried to learn it the best I could. When it was my turn to sing for the director, I gave it all I had, but the strained look that came over his face gave me a clue. He seemed to be trying to understand who was this girl and what happened to the one who sang for him last week?

After the two Anitas were chosen, some of the other girls cried. I just smiled, laughed, and felt a bit like I had been caught with my hand in the cookie jar. I went home, my mother saw me smiling and happy. She frowned and asked "Mae, you got the part?" All I had to say was, "They changed the song."

I did end up with a part in *West Side Story*. First I tried out for "Anybody's" (that was the character's name). She didn't sing. She was the tomboy who hung around the Jets. One small problem: at 5'8", 140 pounds, I was bigger than the guy they chose to play Riff, the Jets' gang leader. So, I ended up being a member of the Jets' gang's girlfriends. I helped design the costumes.

A Small Push and a Lot of Nerve

"No, I don't know what sickle cell anemia is."

"Then you need to look it up. You're always talking about space exploration, why don't you think about something else?"

I hate it when she does that. Whenever my mother

wants me to try something, she doesn't tell me what it is or what to do, she just drops it on the table like a loaf of bread and she leaves. You can pick it up and eat it if you want or you can starve. Your choice. Not a lot of preamble, no warning, at least that I pay attention to. No real direction, and the older I get, the less direction and the more challenge, doubt of my abilities, seems implicit in that casually dropped phrase or topic.

So there it was. Sickle cell anemia. Dropped on the metaphorical table. A challenge. She wasn't going to tell me. Since I think I'm so cool and science smart, a junior in high school, I should know. *Phooey.* She did this just because I said I want to do a science project. Just because I don't want to work anymore with the goldfish swimming in mazes after being exposed in varying concentrations of thyroxin. So what if the cats constantly went fishing in bowls of fish that were scattered throughout the breakfast room. I always cleaned up the goldfish flipping and lying gasping on the floor. I know it costs a lot to buy the goldfish. Okay, the project was a bit of a bummer — their little fish brains had a problem with mazes. But I did do a lot of research on pyridoxine and the effects of thyroid hormone on learning; and I learned how to build a maze with epoxy and acrylic pieces.

Oh, well, this year, sickle cell anemia. I just peeked, it's still just lying on that psychological table. No clues left behind. Why did she do that? I don't know. Maybe to make my work harder than the challenges school provided. I couldn't even gloat and say I knew what sickle cell anemia was.

So do some *research*. The dictionary says "sickle cell anemia is an inherited blood disease found primarily in people of African ancestry." Okey dokey. What do I do now?

I was fifteen and believed and was confident that the world and people wanted to help. Or at least I could talk them into helping me. Who could I turn to for help with this? I knew that hematology was the study of blood diseases. I had once been to Cook County Hospital to visit my aunt, so why not call their lab?

"Just do it, Mae."

"Alright, alright."

"I don't have the number."

"So call the operator." I often had these two-sided dialogues with myself.

"There, the phone is ringing. Are you happy? It's not even the hematology lab. It's the main hospital telephone."

"Ask for the hematology lab."

"And what do I say when Hematology answers? I don't . . . Oh, Hello. My name is Mae Jemison, I am a junior at Morgan Park High School and I'm working on a science project . . . Oh, okay. Yes, I would like to speak to the chief hematology lab technician."

"Slow your breathing down. Do not hyperventilate. Just say . . ."

"Yes, my name is Mae Jemison and I am working on a science project on sickle cell anemia. . . . Uh, huh. High school chemistry and biology. Yes, I read a lot and am good at lab work."

"Yes, I have done science projects before. I would like to help."

"Yes, I can come. . . . Next Tuesday at 4:30 p.m. Sure."

"Mother, how do you get to Cook County Hospital?"

I was a little nervous. I had never taken the train and bus alone all the way from the South Side of Chicago to the West Side where Cook County Hospital Hektoen Hematology Labs were located over on Rush Street. In fact, to my recollection I had never traveled to the West Side by train with or without anyone; we always drove over. By the time I took the 112th Street bus from in front of Morgan Park High School to the Dan Ryan Train Station at 95th and State Streets, then transferred to the "el" train and arrived at Rush Street, it was almost 4:30 p.m.

I met the technician on the 8th floor lab, slightly breathless, but profoundly impressed with myself for getting there on time. The technician, a middle-aged African-American man, asked me what I knew about sickle cell and chemistry. At that point I knew sickle cell disease could be fatal by the time a person became a teenager and historically, very few people survived into their twenties with the disease. I also knew that children and people who had it were often ill, got infections, did not grow well, and had episodes of severe pain called "crises" in their joints and internal organs. I knew that the illness got its name because, at times, the red blood cells of people who suffered with it were shaped like sickles or quarter moons instead of circles like normal red blood cells. But I did not know how it was diagnosed or treated. As I sat there this wonderful man told me how they diagnosed sickle cell anemia in the lab. He showed me equipment, quizzed me on pH and making solutions: molar, normal, and volumetric. I did know some chemistry. I could tell he was impressed. He told me I should come in twice a week.

Over the next month, the technician taught me how to recognize the difference between the electrophoretic movement (how molecules move under the influence of electricity) of normal or A hemoglobin, sickle cell or S hemoglobin, fetal or F hemoglobin. I learned what the pattern looked like that indicated a person had sickle cell anemia, sickle cell trait, normal hemoglobin, thalassemia, or sickle cell and thalassemia combined. (Hey, I know the words are big. But I had to look them up, so you should give it a try, too.) I made solutions for the entire laboratory and set up the electrophoresis chambers. I also learned to do the preliminary test to see if it was even necessary to test the blood sample for hemoglobinopathies. (That's abnormal hemoglobin for those of you not in the know. Now that I was learning how to use these big words, I was *tres* cool.) The lab tech was very impressed with how quickly I learned. So was I — within a month I had the jargon and the swagger.

Then one day, while standing next to the centrifuge, waiting for it to spin down so I could remove a sample, I looked up and there was this white, fortyish, male doctor looking at me. In fact, he was standing over me waiting for me to turn around.

I casually took my samples out of the centrifuge and said hello. He introduced himself as the head of the hematology department. He had a German/Swedish sounding accent. (I couldn't distinguish any further, though I could recognize French, Spanish, British, Southern, East Indian, and nasal Midwestern twang.) He politely inquired who I was and what I was doing in the lab.

Not being overly timid, I answered with my name and politely stated that I was working on a project on sickle cell anemia. I don't recall if he smiled or not, but the next words are imprinted on my memory. He asked quite simply, "What is your hypothesis?"

For the second time in this particular science project adventure, someone, not even my mother this time, had me at a loss for words. After moving my mouth and trying to find an answer, I said I was doing a demonstration project. I knew how to do all this lab work. The doctor replied "No. If you are going to work in my lab on a science project, you will have to get a hypothesis, do more background research, and experimentation." He relieved me of my samples, gave them to one of the lab techs and took me to his office. We discussed a bit more of my background and what a science experiment entailed. Of course I knew about hypotheses and the experimental method. I just didn't have one. He gave me assignments to look up a couple of authors and scientific papers, and to contact the National Institutes of Health. I had to collect more information on the biochemistry of sickle cell anemia in order to determine a compound that might reverse sickling.

I look back now and wonder if I had been set up all along. The head of the hematology department had another student working in the lab on blood typing; he also did not appear to be a person who did not know what was going on in his lab. Over the next months, I spent hours, Saturdays and Sundays at the Illinois Institute of Technology library. I wrote to the National Institutes of Health and they wrote back to me and sent scientific papers! I struggled through original scientific articles that discussed theories about why cells sickled, why the sickle cell trait could sometimes be dangerous, and the effects of low concentrations of oxygen and temperatures on hemoglobin S. These were the circumstances under which the red blood cells changed shape. And I learned that Dr. Linus Pauling, called the father of modern day biochemistry, earned the

Nobel Prize for his work showing that sickle cell anemia disease was caused by the substitution of a single valine amino acid molecule in the sixth position of the normal hemoglobin amino acid sequence. That single substitution causes all the problems. Through this discovery, Dr. Pauling was able to demonstrate that it is the linear sequence of amino acids that determines the 3-D shape of a protein and its physiologic function. Cool. And I didn't know people actually studied black folks' disease. Here was one study fundamental to understanding modern biochemistry.

Through discussion with the physician, I decided on a compound to test that might inhibit sickling. And we tested it! All of this information I had to find and digest. Many times I had to learn other stuff just to really understand one sentence in a medical journal article. I was jazzed!

Then the head of hematology demanded to see my exhibit for the science fair. He also required me to write and type (no computers or word processors available in those days) a scientific paper. It was most embarrassing when he, a non-native speaker of English once corrected my spelling — I bet him and lost. I learned about art transfer letters, how to get photographs from microscopes, and statistics. Whew! He was tough and did not accept "pretty" good. He expected excellence. Period. Nothing less. I was surprised that this European doctor showed so much interest in my work, and allowed me to work in his lab. He seemed to really want me to work in his lab. While I was occasionally intimidated by his knowledge and the task, I always spoke up and would try even harder to be prepared the next time. At fourteen and fifteen, I was comfortable being accepted as his colleague.

Perhaps the most lasting impression of this experience is that my taking a chance of being hung up on, refused, and failing, put me in touch with people willing to take that same chance on me. Sucking up my feelings of "Wow, can I do this?" and just trying, risking, and being willing to put in the effort to accomplish the task led the way to one of the most positive and enabling experiences in my entire life.

Oh, yeah. I almost forgot about what started all of this. What happened at the science fair? I got an "Excellent" at the City Wide Chicago Public School Science Fair. As a result I was invited to an exhibit at a city-wide private school science fair as the public school representative and I won first place.

Student Council: "Y'all are with me, right?"

I really pushed the limits my senior year in the student council with the homecoming parade. Yet I didn't realize until years later, that it was the roadblocks placed by an adult "adversary" that I had to clear which led to our success.

I could not believe our faculty advisor was scolding us. After all the hard work and fun everyone had had. The way the pieces of the puzzle all came together. We had the right to celebrate. To me, it seemed our faculty advisor was just upset because we pulled it off without him, while he had stood back and thought that we — translate me — would fall on our faces.

My answer was, "Mr. O'Bannon, do not stand in here and say these things to *my* student council. If you have any problems you talk to me." I said this in front of everyone. Isn't that what a leader is supposed to do? Stand up for the troops and take the flak?

The other students swiveled their necks back and forth, as they looked at me standing up to Mr. O'Bannon, the vice-principal in charge of student council. Mr. O'Bannon and I always had problems. A black man in his forties, he even recruited a white male student to run against me for student council president. (Interestingly enough the boy he chose was one of my friends; he said his heart wasn't in it.) I do not know why I did not get along with him. Mr. O'Bannon liked my sister, who had been student council president three years before. He is even friends with my brother now. But me, no way.

I still could write hall passes for students. I guess Mr. O'Bannon knew that I would never help anyone cut class. That rigid, principled backbone inside of me went both ways, and as a teenager I applied it ruthlessly.

Which brought us to today's situation. I was indignant that he was not saying "A job well done," but rather seemed to berate us because we did it without him. In fact, the whole thing was pulled off in an impossibly short amount of time, with occasions of how shall we say — not particular grace.

Sometime in the early fall, during our student council class period, the idea of a homecoming parade came up. It sounded wonderful. But it got even better when Mr. O'Bannon said "No way." So, of course we insisted. Then he said he would have nothing to do with it. Even better. I loved good antagonism, back then at fifteen. As a teenager, it was easier to put people in strict categories of good or bad. Looking back I realize it is extraordinary that Mr. Bannon allowed us to attempt holding a parade, when it was against his better judgement. He must have had a certain faith in us and was willing to let us learn the lesson that was awaiting us. I appreciate the patience required to deal effectively with individuals as they search for the limits of their capabilities and others' tolerance. It was important that I had safe outlets for my rebellious leanings.

Football season. I loved football. I even had a football uniform for games: blue jeans, a kelly green shirt, kelly green derby, tons of school pins on the shirt, gray Hush Puppy tie up shoes, and a white nylon jacket. Morgan Park's colors were green and white. The team's mascot was the Mustang. I had green-and-white pom-poms left over from my freshman and sophomore years as a pom-pom girl.

Homecoming parade. Sounds great! What do we have to do? Floats, marching band, decorations. We can ask the shop and art classes to help out. We'll need to raise money. What else? To Mr. O'Bannon's credit, he would raise stumbling blocks about problems that needed to be solved when we didn't even know the problems existed. An example: Who knew you needed a parade permit?

So one day, Lynda Bundrage, my best friend and the vice president of student council, Jimmy Sparks, a friend with a car, and I found ourselves downtown on our way to city hall. It was a football game day at Morgan Park. Jimmy Sparks was about 6'2", maybe weighed 140 pounds soaking wet, and he was the drum major of the school band. He was dressed in his drum major uniform; I, of course, had on my green-and-white football outfit and Lynda was dressed for football, too.

Chicago is known as the Windy City and the wind was howling down Michigan Avenue that day. As we walked down the street, the tails of Jimmy's white drum major jacket flapped in the wind. Lynda struggled to keep up because Jimmy and I walked quickly toward city hall to apply for the parade permit. When we arrived, all windblown, the clerk there asked us if we were dressed for Halloween. When you're with two other people, hey, what's humiliation?

FINDING A PLACE

For me, the most peculiar aspect of being a teenager and going to an integrated high school in Chicago in the early seventies did not center around "finding myself." I knew who I was. I knew about as well as anyone with swirling hormones, increasing shoe sizes, and shifting family status, and responsibilities can. Rather, the peculiar part was not allowing others — adults and students, blacks and whites — to stick me inside a particular box just to make it easier for them to categorize me. If they could, then they would not have to see, talk to, respond, and deal with me, the individual.

I tended to complicate the box problem a bit more for people. I was a feminist, and excelled in and aspired to careers in both science and dance. I was outspoken. I was basically happy, forgiving, moderately well-read, not a "druggie," and willing to take stands and risks.

For example, I went from being the darling of the advanced placement U.S. history class when we studied the policies of *laissez-faire* to the teacher's major provocateur and class hell-raiser as we approached slavery and the modern era. In fact, my friends said that they came to class to see the "Mae and Mr. Meade Show."

My friends reflected my range of interests and the many places I felt comfortable. Here is the rundown on my high school posse, "homeys," friends, gang, buddies, whatever. Not listed in any particular order.

Kathy Sharpe and I were an unlikely pair. Kathy was a blue-eyed platinum blonde, and stocky, about 5'1".

Kathy and I took Russian together for four years, were pom-pom girls our freshman and sophomore years. Kathy could usually get her family car and we'd drive around in the evenings always ending up at White Castle on 127th Street and Western Avenue in Blue Island to buy hamburgers and onion rings. Kathy and I talked about all kinds of things from boys, ones we liked,

Childhood

1956. I'm snuggled all tight and cozy in Daddy's arms, while Ada Sue is up front and center at our home in Decatur, Alabama.

1961. Ricky (7), me (4), and Ada Sue (8) stand in front of the house next door in Chicago. See the stairs? They make a great stoop!

1973. My high school graduation picture, taken at age 15, reflects my personality and the styles of the time: Afros, large hoop earrings, and the medallions with African markings. (My brother gave me this one.) The smile is all mine.

School

1973. Front row, from left to right: Tony Green, Lynda Bundrage, me, and Sheila Wang with the Morgan Park High School Student Council.

1973. Back row, middle: That's me, in my high school Modern Dance Club. Senior year I helped choreograph lots of dances. I was president of this club as well as of the Russian Club.

1977. My mother and father came to California for my graduation from Stanford University. Ada Sue took a week off from medical school and came, too. I had a great time showing them all around the San Francisco Bay Area.

1981. Joan Culpepper and I made it! Graduation from Cornell as full fledged MDs!

Abroad

1979. Here I am, laughing as usual, and posing with one of the nursing sisters I worked with on the Embu District community health diagnosis project in Kenya, the summer after my second year in medical school.

1985. The Cairo Museum in Egypt overflows with ancient artifacts— from huge statues like this one I am standing in front of, to mummies, jewels, and papyrus.

Astronaut Training

1987. Fifteen people entered NASA's astronaut program. The ASCANs (Astronaut Candidates) came from different places across the United States and had different skills. By the end of our first year, when we all received our astronaut pins, we had learned tons about spacecraft, orbital dynamics, planetology, and how the human body adjusts to weightlessness, aerodynamics, the space shuttle, NASA — and each other.

1987. Astronauts fly and train in two-seater, supersonic T-38 jets. We took survival training to learn what to do if there was a problem and we had to eject from the airplane.

1987. Training to use a parachute: I'm going to be pulled off this boat and up a couple hundred feet in the air — followed by a drop down into the ocean.

1987. Survival training in the woods in Washington state, I learned to use the emergency radio and compass to guide rescuers to my location.

1992. I trained for my flight on Spacelab J at this full-size, high-fidelity simulator at Marshall Spaceflight Center in Huntsville, Alabama. I am wearing equipment for one of the experiments called Autogenic Feedback Training—learning to control my body's reaction to the stresses of spaceflight.

1988. Simulators are machines, panels, and sometimes whole rooms that simulate how equipment operates. NASA has many simulators to practice everything from stowing your clothes and flying the shuttle to taking space walks. Astronauts learn on all of them. I first learned about all the systems and switches common to space shuttles on simulators like this one.

1992. My second official NASA astronaut photo taken about four months before my spaceflight. I am in the orange launch and entry suit that is worn during liftoff and landing.

Space

1992. Space, the real thing! On board the space shuttle *Endeavour*, I am starting an IV on a fake hand to ensure that it can be done and that the amount of fluid a person receives can accurately be controlled in weightlessness. Up there you cannot drip the fluid because things don't fall. You actually have to pump it. Oh yeah, I made the IV solutions using water that formed when our oxygen and hydrogen fuel cells created electricity for the space shuttle.

1992. On launch pad 39A at Kennedy Space Center, at the Terminal Countdown Demonstration Test for Spacelab J two weeks before the mission. Looking down you can see the white solid rocket booster and the large rust colored external tank. The *Endeavour* shuttle is protected by a "building" that is moved away just hours before launch.

1992. After landing at Kennedy Space Center, all the crew did a "walk-down" of the shuttle. Still a little wobbly from the extreme changes in environments (weightlessness to lots of weight) we still take time to notice any wear and tear on the shuttle after its three- million-mile journey. From left to right: Mamoru Mohri, me, Jay Apt, Curt Brown, Hoot Gibson, Jan Davis, and Mark Lee.

1992. Linda Lorelle, NBC-KPRC Houston evening news anchor, interviews me at Ellington Field immediately after returning to Houston from the *Endeavour* landing at Kennedy Space Center. Actually, Linda is my best friend from Stanford University. Here we are, both grown-up, doing our jobs.

1992. With Nichelle Nichols, aka Lt. Uhura, in Los Angeles after my spaceflight. She presented me with the Johnson Publishing Trail Blazers Award for 1992.

1993. *Star Trek* crew Geordi La Forge and Lt. Palmer at the transport station aboard the Starship *Enterprise*. Actually, it's LeVar Burton and me in Starfleet uniforms when I appeared in the *Star Trek: The Next Generation* episode "Second Chances."

Where the Wind Goes

1997. I continue to pass on my hope for the future and encourage teenagers around the world to explore and understand through The Earth We Share international science camp. Here participant Sheila Wong-Shue and I are at the 1997 camp at Dartmouth College.

1989. On top of the planetarium in Rio de Janeiro, Brazil, I was pleased to share my love of the sky with small children there.

those who didn't give us a second look; and teachers; to more philosophical things like science fiction and what the world would be like in the future. I learned to play Ping-Pong at Kathy's house. Her little brother was fun sometimes, but mostly omnipresent and irritating. (Was that what I was like to my brother and sister?) Once while walking with Kathy down my block on the way to her house, we passed an older black teenage boy sitting on his porch. He asked me why didn't I hang with my own kind. My block had changed from all white to primarily black in the three years since my family first integrated it. Funny, I thought, Kathy was my kind. She was a smart, athletic, courageous, and out-of-the-box thinking young woman like me. Without being naïve, certainly Kathy was at least as close to "my kind" as he was.

I met Kathy at Esmond Elementary School, but we became close friends in high school. I heard from her frequently when she first went off to college. Recently I received a note from her. She majored in Forestry in college and for a while was a forest ranger. Absolutely my kind.

Once the dress code requiring girls to wear skirts and dresses was eliminated, Sheila Wang and I were the two girls in school who were never seen in anything but pants. Sheila's dad was from China and her mother was a white American. Sheila and I were political rebels in our class and were both quite good in math and science. In fact, my senior year, each morning at 7 a.m. before classes started, Mr. Drymiller met with us to teach us solid analytic geometry and calculus. At the end of our junior year class in Algebra III and Trigonometry, Mr. Drymiller offered to teach us the advanced mathematics we would need to know as we entered the universities we would probably attend. We jumped at the chance. At the time I did realize what a special effort Mr. Drymiller had made. But later I understood just how important his effort was to my academic and professional development. And truly, how incredible it was for a teacher to give so much of his time. Sheila received her Ph.D. in Physiological Psychology about four years ago. She is the mother of three teenage children.

Denise Thomas also known as Dee Dee. New York trial lawyer and co-developer of the off-Broadway musical *A Brief History of White Music in America*. The musical features popular white music hits over the years from "How Much is that Doggie in the Window" to "I Wanna Hold Your Hand" but sung by black singers. It's great music with a fresh, enlightening twist to an old theme, it demonstrates in an entertaining way how white singers made hits off black music — think Elvis, Pat Boone, and the Rolling Stones. That's Dee Dee. Dee Dee, then a thin — actually skinny in high school — tall African-American high school student who was spirited, smart and just straight up fun. Today? Well, some things never change.

Famous Mae and Dee Dee story. Senior year we were in the same English class taught by my homeroom teacher of four years, Mrs. Roberts. Mrs. Roberts and I had been mutual admirers for all that time. For example, I was the first girl ever to sign up for drafting class at Morgan Park and Mr. Okelpek, the drafting teacher, came to ask her about me; Mrs. Roberts assured him I was sincere. Mr. Okelpek learned that I wanted to be an engineer and he made sure I was well exposed to engineering drawings. He was pretty cool, too.

I only lived a couple blocks from school, but I was occasionally late to class. In fact, I had several tardy slips. One morning, I passed Dee Dee in the hallway as she went to get a late slip. I thought, maybe, just maybe Mrs. Roberts will take pity on me. So, I continued to class. Approximately one minute after the bell rang, I walked into the classroom. Mrs. Roberts smiled and told me to sit down. I took my assigned seat right in front of her desk, and class continued. We discussed the novel the class was currently reading. However, my neck began to tingle. I felt dirty looks and arrows slung from the students sitting behind me. It was no different than usual. I always did my homework and would "help the class out" with the answers whenever Mrs. Roberts asked me to. Was I an "apple polisher"? No, I don't think so. Yeah, it was honors English and many other students just did not answer because it was Mrs. Roberts, and they didn't like her. But, hey, I did and she was my homeroom teacher. You cannot antagonize everyone and survive and live long and prosper.

Dee Dee walked into the room about two minutes after I did, handed Mrs. Roberts a tardy slip, glared at me and sat down. The intensity of the darts, arrows, and dirty looks flung in my direction intensified. What's the problem? I haven't answered any more questions or smiled more ingratiatingly than usual. Y'all know me, I'm right there with you to mock Mr. Meade and Mr. O'Bannon. But, to Mrs. Roberts I am goodness and light. You know I suck up to Mrs. Roberts, but I can't alienate all the teachers. It is not my intent to. After all, Mrs. Branecki even made me a gym leader my junior year, instead of waiting for my senior year even after I got a D in gym in freshman year.

Everyone confronted me after class. "I can't believe it." "Don't you have any dignity?" "You came in after Dee Dee." "She made Dee Dee go get a tardy slip. She told you 'Welcome, Mae.'" I smiled sheepishly and said nothing.

I ask you, what should I have done? Volunteered to keep solidarity with Dee Dee, a fellow student, and gotten the fifth tardy that would have required my parents to come up to school? Or go with the flow? Dee Dee, I rest my case.

Actually, I didn't get the most flak about the tardy slip and Mrs. Roberts from Dee Dee, but from Tony Green and Lynda Bundrage — my aces. The three of us hung out all the time and if you found one you could always find the others. We were like the Three Musketeers. We were totally cool and at the same time, three of the most "un-hip" people. Tony had a Datsun that he drove to school, so unless Lynda and I irritated him, we generally had wheels. Lynda was Miss Cutie Pie who was always perfectly dressed, coifed, and tried to be grown up.

For some reason Lynda and Tony thought they could sing. So they formed this group called "The Sands of Time" and convinced Dee Dee to join. Dee Dee, however, could sing. I didn't feel left out because I knew I couldn't sing. It wasn't until I went to Tony's house to watch them practice that I found out they couldn't sing either. It was pitiful.

My high school career can be summarized by the following paradoxes. (If you don't know the word, look it up.)

1. I got the award for academic achievement in English instead of in Science. The paradox was that I was not particularly known as an English maven, although I did get all A's. Science was what I was known for, and I was the only student from my high school to consistently enter and win awards in science fairs including city-wide science fairs. I scored very high on the math and physics SAT tests. I received scholarship offers from MIT, Rensselaer Polytechnic Institute, and Bell Labs, as well as from Stanford. And yes, I got all A's in science as well.

2. After being voted "Most Popular," "Most Likely to Succeed," and being elected student council president, I threw a post-graduation barbeque with the girl voted "Sexiest" (Lynda Bundrage) and my male "Most Popular" (Tony Green) counterpart. But no one came. We sent out

invitations weeks in advance. On the other hand, my sister Ada Sue had a small party announced on a day she was not at school, and our house was so crowded with invitees and crashers, folks were angry when they were turned away.

A Last Breath of Adolescence

"Okay, Mother, please let me go. I'll be going off to college in a month anyway. It'll be me, Lynda, Tony, and and Tony's little cousin and his grandparents. It'll be safe. Please?"

"I don't know."

"Please say yes!"

"Okay, but just the weekend."

"So you all, I can go to Idylwild, Michigan. But you know to keep your cousin away from me. I do not like little, bad, noisy kids."

That's what the summer after high school and that dud graduation party was like. Tony, Lynda, and me hanging out. I had a summer job. I helped the Morgan Park administrator in the Pupil Employment Program sponsored out of the Mayor's Office of the City of Chicago. By the time the summer program came to an end, I was responsible for doing payroll, keeping attendance, and finding placement for the other students. During the day, I learned how to talk people into hiring students, I decided if there really was a job at their location, tattled on poorly performing placement sites to the director, and calculated hours and salaries.

In the evening Tony, Lynda, and I would go to the drive-in movies. We were not particularly good neighbors. Yes, we did disturb the folks in the cars next to us with our continuous commentary on the action, heroine, hero, implausibility of the plot, coolness, etc. Come on, with movies like *The Mack, Coffy*, and *Tales from the Crypt*, you *gotta* talk. Sometimes folks in the neighboring cars became irritated with us, like the time I said "I'm gonna close my eyes" during a scary film, and a *BIG* woman in the car next to me said "I wish you would close your mouth." Or, when we had to move the car to another space and sneak to the concession stand because the guy in the car next to us threatened to kick Tony's butt, if he didn't stop talking. Tony with his "no fighting self" lipped off. We had to make a fast exit.

Back to Idylwild. Idylwild, Michigan, was where we Three Musketeers were going to spend one last fun-filled three-day weekend. We would soon be going our separate ways. Tony to Hampton Institute in Virginia, Lynda to Spelman College in Atlanta, and me to Stanford University in Palo Alto, California. We were all changing, even then.

Here was the proposition: Tony's grandparents had a house in the country. A country fair was scheduled there over the weekend. All we had to do was to pick up Tony's disorderly little cousin Daryl and drive up in Tony's grandparents' car. (Not his trademark green Datsun. By the way, Tony owned a lot of green stuff, as his name was Tony Green. Childish, square, yes, but it worked for him.) Simple enough plan if Daryl was kept away from me, and Lynda didn't get too prissy in the woods.

Great first step: We all made it to Michigan. I hadn't put Daryl out on a strip of lonely highway 50 miles outside of Chicago. We lugged Lynda's suitcase full of new, cute clothes and deposited them in the house. Tony and I grabbed our small bags. We went to our rooms and since it was night time, and pitch-black outside, we went to sleep.

Bright and early the following morning we took Tony's grandparents' car and went into town after eating breakfast. There was the carnival, with rides, gaming booths, cotton candy, and homemade ice cream, all kinds of flavors of ice cream. Tony and I ate until we were sick. We waited in line for this ride called the Hammer, which was two large cages on the end of large struts that just swung around a pivot point. During the ride, we were scared silly, screaming, and embarrassing ourselves. Upon exiting the Hammer, we looked at each other, terror and tears in our eyes, and said, "Gotta go again." Back in line we went.

All day, Lynda hung away from us, a bit aloof. We noticed that she didn't laugh at our jokes as much. She didn't appreciate it when we goosed her. Lynda seemed to be getting all stuffy and prissy in preparation to go to a sophisticated all-women's college. I still couldn't believe she was going to an all girls' school.

Tony and I kept behaving childishly and having lots of fun.

He commented on Lynda wearing a chic pair of large dark sunglasses. She was acting particular, proper, and very adult, like the sophisticated twin on *The Patty Duke Show*. So that's what Tony called her: "Patty Duke."

Needless to say, Lynda didn't appreciate it. By this time, we were exhausted, broke, and had teased Lynda until she was extremely perturbed with us. So we all climbed into the car to go home. I offered Miss Duke the front seat with Tony. She'd had enough of us and jumped in the back. Just as Tony was starting up the car, a spider scurried across the back seat. Lynda screamed bloody murder and asked us to kill it. Tony howled with laughter. I said, "That little spider can't do anything to a great big old you." Patty Duke commanded that we kill it, *now.* I said, "Oh no, not me." Tony smiled and said it was getting closer. Lynda replied, "Oh, I wish you two would just grow up." Unfortunately for Lynda, we did not grow up that weekend and the spider stayed alive and seated comfortably next to her. That fact made our day. But of course, we had to grow up later.

THERE'S A CHANGE IN THE AIR

Boys/Crushes

Leroy. Leroy was the first real boy that I *liked*. Real boy. You know, besides my twenty-year-old second cousin, who didn't count. I don't even remember Leroy's last name, but I had a big crush on him, and I think he liked me, too. I spent a wonderful summer with him in fourth-grade summer school. I can remember much of it vividly. He was brown-skinned with a short haircut. He was quite cute and all the girls liked him. We were about the same height. He was smart, too. *Almost* as smart as me. He may have even known some things I didn't, and he had nice legs.

Fourth-grade summer school. Usually, Leroy went to Fermi Elementary School. He was attending my school, Alexandre Dumas Elementary, just for summer school. We really didn't even live in the same neighborhood. He was the first and last boy for a long time that I didn't mind talking to. In fact I liked talking to him and got butterflies in my stomach around him. He liked the fact that I had a natural hairstyle, when many of the other kids made fun of me. For girls, it was not cool to have nappy hair at that time, especially short nappy hair, but Leroy liked it. We worked on projects together and sat next to each other in class. I only saw him one time after summer school. He walked over to my street. I saw him while I was playing jump rope after school one day. I was so excited to see him. If only I could just talk to him a little while, but I couldn't act too interested for two reasons. First, if Ada Sue and Ricky saw, I would never be able to live it down; second, I wasn't allowed to play with boys by myself.

Actually I could not go out on an official date with boys until I was sixteen years old. I turned sixteen in October of my senior year in high school! So, while skipping seventh grade was great academically, and in some ways socially, too, I was still behind my classmates.

That's okay, because I didn't really start to *like* boys until I was fourteen anyway and again it happened at summer school. I almost always went to summer school, because I couldn't bear not to be busy and I loved learning. This time I took chemistry at Kenwood High School in Hyde Park. I wanted to take as much science as I could, as soon as I could. I couldn't wait until my senior year of high school. That particular summer was memorable not only because I met DC, but also because I repaid my brother big time for his stunts when I was younger. If I say so myself, it was one of my best moves. I'll chronicle it later.

Oh, it's too good, let me tell it now. As teenage siblings, though we were allies outside the house, at home Ricky and I had numerous ongoing conflicts. From wearing one another's clothing without permission to cleaning the dog poop out of the yard to fighting over my blackmailing him regarding classified, secret girlfriends. There was always tension between us. I really don't remember what got this particular battle started, but I successfully ended it.

Ricky had really made me mad the night before, and he got the last lick in. At seventeen he was bigger than I was, but I could now give him a run for his money. This time I proposed if he didn't leave me alone I would put a hole in his waterbed. It was an idle threat and we both knew it. It was too destructive and would get me into serious trouble with the greater powers that be, my parents. Knowing that idle threats were self-defeating, I had to think of something else, a substantive way to follow through. The solution came to me in the night. I knew how to execute it and make a clean getaway. I would carry out the retribution as I walked out the door to catch the bus at seven in the morning. My father would be home then to block any brutal retaliations. After the long trip to Kenwood High School, I would be over fifty blocks away. Ample distance would then separate me from Ricky.

Morning came and I dressed while Ricky snoozed. My mother and father, who were always up early to go to work, were already in the kitchen. I quietly put my books and bag by the door and unlocked it. My heart pounded rapidly in my chest. My arms felt watery, my stomach churned. Timing was everything. It would be close. I calmly walked to the kitchen and filled a large soup kettle with ice and water. I went to my father to get lunch money and to let him see that I was fully dressed and ready for school. The pieces were in place. Nothing was left but the execution.

I picked up my weapon and went quietly to Ricky's

room. Flinging open the door, I called his name. Half-open eyes stared up at me from a deep sleep. Realization slowly dawned and his eyes bucked. He shouted, "Mae, you better not . . ." just as the ice-cold water, soup pot, and everything splashed across his face and body, soaking his bed clothes.

He jumped out of bed quickly, but I was faster. I grabbed my books and bag and was out the door as I heard my father say, "Boy, you better leave that girl alone." Sheer perfection. I walked, skipped actually, down the two sunlit blocks to the bus stop, to Kenwood, chemistry, and DC.

DC was tall, muscular, and going into his senior year. He was in my chemistry class. He was the quarterback for our arch-rival football team, Chicago Vocational High School (CVS). My school, Morgan Park, was one of the few integrated public high schools in Chicago, and it was also considered a school where the goody two-shoes, college prep, and middle-class kids went. CVS on the other hand, had a reputation for some tough kids. It was twice as big as Morgan Park back then. In fact, at the football games between the Morgan Park Mustangs and the CVS Cavaliers, Morgan Park students were always let out of the stadium first. This gave us a head start to get on the bus, into cars, or just get some "hat" — get away as quickly as possible. This was particularly important if we won and chants of "Humbug, Humbug" after the game echoed from the other side of the stadium, challenging our opponents to a fight. (I must add, just for pride's sake, that Morgan Park was not the biggest wimp in the Red Division South football league. Actually, we used to chant "Humbug, Humbug" after the game to Bogan High School. Of course we never did anything, but we were held, while they left early.)

As occasional lab partners that summer, I learned a lot about DC and his pride for CVS. Contrary to my preconceptions concerning handsome, muscular football players, he was very intelligent, disciplined, and willing to follow my lead. But you know, willing or not, I was going to *take* the lead in science class. I was impressed by the fact that he was very conscientious about measurements and how he recorded his experimental results. I didn't feel compelled to check his work. In fact he was possibly more meticulous than I was. No, I am not and was not obsessive, I just wanted things to be correct. It was my lab grade as well. DC and I had discussions about all kinds of things. He lived with his mother and worked after school. He was a member of the ROTC.

Surprisingly, DC liked me also. I say surprisingly because though I knew I had a face grown-ups thought was pretty, I never really dressed up. I always wore pants. People occasionally still called me son, because of my short hair. But, it didn't bother me as I was having too much fun with ballet and modern dance classes, science fairs, plays, pom-pom girls, riding my bicycle, reading, harassing my brother, student politics, museums, whatever; besides there would be time for boys later. It even embarrassed me a bit to like boys. Shhh, I didn't want my parents to know. And definitely not my brother or sister, since I had made their dating lives miserable every chance I got, in that annoying little sister kind of way. DC and I spent lots of time talking in class; occasionally we would take the same bus on the way home. But we never went on a date in high school. We exchanged our phone numbers and addresses and stayed in contact. He went to the United States Naval Academy in Annapolis, Maryland. That was my first introduction to military academies. (At that time these academies did not accept women which I thought was bogus.) DC and I continued to write each other and keep abreast of one another's lives. We later dated a few times after my freshman and sophomore years at Stanford.

That's it, no more stories, otherwise I will have to change the names to protect the innocent, the guilty, the trifling, the wonderful, and those who don't know they were targeted but missed. I definitely did okay, had my heart broken a few times, and may have reciprocated on others. But I am here, healthy and happy.

Here's my one "I'm older than you, I've been through this, just trust me" piece of advice. Take the high school and college romance, boy/girl stuff, with a huge grain of salt. Why? Because first, at that stage in life, very few people actually know what they want. Those who believe they do, often want something or someone that is not appropriate or beneficial for them. As a young adult, you are still learning not only about the world but about yourself at a very fast pace; with any luck you will continue to learn things about yourself, your career, likes, dislikes, and just plain new stuff. More likely than not, that college boy or girl will not be the love of your life and probably will not be around except, if you're lucky, as a friend in one or two years. I know it's true — a few lucky couples do last and build a wonderful life together — but it's not the norm. And finally, boy-friends and girlfriends always, always seem to mess up in some way close to finals or important midterms. They're not malicious, it's probably just the stress.

Now, whether it's the star running back, the neurotic drop-outs, engineering majors, political scientists, or theologians I can say without going into details, without hesitation, from my experience, and the experiences of my friends and classmates, male and female, these are good words of advice. Heed them. I wish someone had given me a hint earlier.

ENCOUNTERS WITH
THE SANTA ANA

Moving to "The Farm"

I was nervous, excited, lonely, sad, and happy all at the same time. I was sixteen years old, standing in O'Hare Airport with my parents, waiting to board a plane for San Francisco, California. I was on my way to Stanford University, by myself. I had never seen the campus. Neither I nor anyone in my immediate family had ever been to California before.

I was wearing a maroon, wool shirt jacket that I made, a turtleneck, and jeans. It was toward the end of September in Chicago, and still fairly warm. My suitcase contained a number of outfits, mostly pants, that I had diligently sewn during the previous two weeks. I usually made my own clothes back then. I could sew exactly what I wanted and it was cheaper to buy good cloth and have well-made clothing than getting things from the stores. The trunk that I had mailed ahead to Stanford had all my heavy duty items: an iron, new towels, blankets, black-and-white polka-dot sheets, a small black-and-white television set, boots, my coats and winter clothes, and the books I wanted with me.

My mother, father, and I had spent the last three weeks preparing for college. It felt like old hat because this was really our third time; we were all involved when my sister and brother went off to school. But this time I was leaving. I spent most of the money I made from summer work and local academic awards buying my college stuff. I was proud that I had been able to buy myself a TV and new gray Hush Puppies shoes. I still had about $200 of my own to take with me to open a checking account. I had never had a checking account before, but I was confident I could handle it, I had always watched my mother balance hers.

My mother looked sad. My father was stoic. I was determined not to cry, after all I hadn't cried in over four years, but I was leaving home. I had always looked forward to going away to school. This was something I had to go through in life. I was going to exactly the school I wanted. I was embarking on a career in engineering, and would have teachers, rather professors, who would challenge me and mentor me in a science career. And I was going to *California*, the heart of new things and innovation, radical politics and cool science. Stanford University, known as "The Farm," was the first school to have coed dorms with girls and boys on the same floor. They were written up in *Esquire* magazine.

As boarding time came closer, I began to worry about my parents. What would they do without me? Could they cope? I would write often, it was too expensive to call. I hoped my parents would not worry about me. I would be just fine, after all, I grew up in a big city, and I was smart and healthy.

As the plane began its descent into the San Francisco Bay Area I could see the Sierra Nevada Mountains and the foothills that lead to the Pacific Ocean. It was a brilliant, clear day. The pilot said we would get wonderful views of the Bay Area as we were routed along the peninsula. "Ladies and gentleman, on the left of the plane all those red tile roofs are Stanford University." It came over the speaker. I was actually here. My heart skipped and a big smile came to my face. I'm here.

The instructions on the freshman arrival form said there would be Stanford representatives with signs at baggage claim. After collecting my bags and identifying myself to the Stanford folks I was directed to the place to wait for the Stanford bus. I leaned on the wall — cool, relaxed, and in control, at least that's the appearance I wanted to give. A young man came up and introduced himself as a member of the Stanford Black Student Union (BSU). The BSU was helping to welcome the African-American students and transport them to campus. So I got in the van with a number of other students. The drive down the 101 expressway, (I learned it was called freeway in California) was filled with talk about what to expect and what events the BSU was putting on to welcome students. Many of the students were living in Roble Hall, the Black Theme House. I was not.

We entered Stanford's grounds via Palm Drive. The campus was beautiful. Trees, palm trees, plants, and flowers were everywhere. The air was fresh. The stucco buildings were beige with red tile roofs. The van dropped me off in the parking lot of the Florence Moore Hall Alondra House dormitory. There was a table set up in the parking lot. As I looked around trying to figure out what to do, I heard my name. "Mae." Not possible, I do not know anyone here. Again, "Mae! Up here."

I looked up and saw this young blonde woman leaning out of a window of the second floor, waving. "I'm Janet, your roommate." Janet Waggoner was probably the best roommate I could have had that year. She was 5'10" or 5'11" tall. I was not used to women taller than me. She was nineteen and had spent a year in Sweden as an exchange student. Janet grew up in Oakdale, California, on a ranch in the San Joaquin Valley. She was from a small rural town, I was from the big city. She had a great smile and sunny personality.

I was a bit overwhelmed that Janet had been on the lookout for me. She came downstairs and helped me tote my bags up. We lugged my trunk up the stairs. Then we settled down and talked. She knew all about Stanford. I just knew it had a good engineering school and football team and a bit about the academics. Over the year, Janet and I studied together under the shadow of the Stanford radio telescope dish in the foothills behind campus. We pooled our resources and cooked our meals when the campus food service workers went on strike. I even learned to ride and groom horses at her ranch.

Alondra was a four-class coed dorm. It not only had freshmen, but sophomores, juniors, and seniors. But right then, the only upperclassmen present were our resident assistants, Tammy and John. They got all the freshman together that evening, about twelve to fifteen of us, to brief us on freshman orientation. Tammy was a junior and pre-med major from Southern California and reminded me of the real life version of the Beach Boys song "I wish they all could be California girls." She also drove a Mercedes, which her parents replaced with an Audi, when "The Benz" had mechanical problems. John was a senior pre-med major from Philadelphia. He was intense and funny.

People already knew a lot about each other including about me. They knew I intended to be an engineering major and that I was only sixteen and the youngest person in the dorm. That fact provided endless entertainment throughout the year, but not in a mean-spirited way. For example, when I got a traffic ticket I had to get an adult, someone over eighteen, to go with me to juvenile court since my parents were in Chicago. Ha ha. My dorm mates thought I was pretty cool to be so young and be in college, but, they never treated me any differently.

In our group we had folks from all over the United States, from the East Coast to Birmingham, Alabama, to small towns in Kansas, and, of course, throughout California. We were all excited to be at Stanford.

Linda Jones, also an African-American freshman from Chicago, lived in Alondra. She played tennis (really *well*), spoke French, had been to Europe, and loved to dance. Her father, a pediatrician, and her mother came to California with Linda to help her settle in. Linda and I became great friends. Later, as anchor woman on the Houston evening news, Linda covered my launch in space. True story.

I found camaraderie and support in the dorm. I took part in school activities and dorm shenanigans. One really cool thing was playing intramural football. Did I forget to tell you the real reason I wanted to go to Stanford? Football. I was a football fanatic. Stanford played what was termed "Razzle-Dazzle" football. You know — punt and field goal fakes, lateral-lateral passes. Stanford won the Rose Bowl two years in a row before I arrived. They denied their Big Ten opponent a touchdown or field goal with first down on the one yard line. The football team, the band, and the fans were fun. The four linebackers were called "Thunder Chickens" because they were smaller than a lot of other college football line-backers. Anyway, Stanford football was a big draw for me, *and* they had coed intramural football leagues.

I had never actually played football before. I knew the plays, strategies etc., but I had never played. I was athletic and strong and roughhoused with my brother, so I was definitely game to be on our dorm football team. However I mistakenly thought that to block in touch football, you merely got in the way of the opponent, not really tackle them. Our dorm team was made up of two girls (Tammy and me) and regular guys (read small, not particularly imposing males), and our first game was played against a fraternity team (read big and mean). I learned several things. First, the only time just "touching" counts is with the person carrying the ball, otherwise you get bumped. Second, some guys will try to intimidate women with their strength. Third, and most importantly, it feels good to make a good, solid hard block. Especially "hitting" a big guy who thought he had you intimidated and thought a girl couldn't stop him. That's fun. During my intramural football career, I sustained the only broken bone I ever had in my life, a hairline fracture of my left index finger when I almost caught a "long bomb." It hurt like crazy, but, I kept playing. This was too much fun!

Being What I Intended To Be

My Leland Stanford, Jr. University Diploma of Graduation reads, *"Conferred on Mae Carol Jemison, who has satisfactorily pursued the studies and passed the examinations required, therefore the Degree of Bachelor of Science with all the rights, privileges and Honors there unto appertaining . . ."* My diploma was signed by the chair of the Chemical Engineering Department and the Dean of the School of Engineering. My formal transcript from Stanford lists my degree as BS Chemical Engineering, and notes *Also fulfilled the requirements for an AB in African and Afro-American Studies."* Stanford did not grant two degrees unless you spent an extra year in residence. I completed the course requirements for both Chemical Engineering and African and Afro-American Studies in four years.

Why I completed two degrees in four years permeates my experience at Stanford, majoring in engineering. Really, it reveals obstacles placed purposefully or accidentally in my path when I intended to be someone who others may not have believed I could or should be.

I arrived at Stanford with the intention of doing an interdepartmental major in biomedical engineering, a new field that I learned about during a two-week program sponsored by the Junior Engineering Technical Society at the University of Illinois in Urbana. I had attended this program prior to my senior year in high school. That summer I was able to reconcile my love of physics, biology, practical implementation, and creativity in this one area of biomedical engineering. When I considered colleges to attend, actually I didn't just look at football teams, but also the engineering schools and interdisciplinary-major possibilities. Being politically and socially aware, I also considered other curricula and benefits offered: Dr. Linus Pauling; the mile long Stanford Linear Accelerator Center; radio telescopes on campus; great engineering, medical, law and business schools; a California location; and a great football team. Stanford University was clearly the hands-down winner.

My goal my first quarter at college was to find an academic advisor in biomedical engineering, continue to become fluent in Russian, which I was convinced would be important in science and space exploration, become involved in dance and athletics, and do well in my classes. I had always gotten along well with and was supported by my teachers. I went to an integrated high school and had scored quite high on the standard academic tests, ACT and SAT, including the physics and math specialty tests. I had received scholarship offers not only from all the schools I applied to, including Massachusetts Institute of Technology, Cornell, and Rensselaer Polytechnic Institute, but also from their alumnae associations. I was confident and outgoing and worked really hard, but I was unprepared for the response I got from my engineering advisor.

Advisees were invited over to Dr. Kline's house. I had never been in one of my teacher's homes before. It was a bit intimidating to be there. I do not remember exactly how many advisees he had, but I do remember I was the only black girl. There were not many other women, and no other blacks. Everyone seemed at ease and friendly. No one spoke to me much, but I tried to join in. People were discussing their schedules, what courses they should take, what courses they tested in or out of.

I had taken four years of Russian in high school, and I was pretty good at it, so I took the Russian placement test. The test and instructions were in Russian, which by the way, has a different alphabet from English. After the test we were told that our advisors would let us know what class to sign up for.

In high school I had taken solid analytic geometry

and calculus. So, trying to join in and be casual like everyone else, I asked my advisor if I should take the accelerated calculus without solid analytic geometry, since I had already had it. He said no, just take the regular calculus for engineering, physics, and math majors. I was a bit surprised that he said this without discussing my background in mathematics. Later that evening I was devastated when I asked how to find out what class to take in Russian. Dr. Kline said, and I remember clearly, "If they have not contacted you, just assume that you should take beginning Russian." I wanted to cry. For the first time in my academic career, here was a teacher, a professor, who was supposed to help me, telling me twice in one evening that I had learned little in high school. He doubted me without bothering to learn anything about me. I worried, I must really not be as bright as everyone was telling me and as my scores seemed to reflect, if after four years I could not place out of first quarter Russian.

As silly as it may seem now, and as silly as it seemed to me my junior and senior year at Stanford, I was actually too embarrassed to go to the Russian Language Department to find the real answer. I was too embarrassed to let them know I had taken four years of Russian, but still might be in the beginning class. Consequently, I never took Russian at Stanford.

When I started at Stanford, I had a very easy smile. In fact I smiled and was so optimistic, that I remember one senior, a gorgeous black woman with a short natural called me "Smiley." Though she was not a science major she cautioned me not to take too seriously what some folks would say about my intended course of study in engineering. For example, one African-American pre-med junior called "Wild Bill" advised me that no African Americans had passed Calculus 41A the first time. I did not take his advice to heart, but began to realize that if I was to make it in engineering I would probably have to make it on my own.

There were other African-American students majoring in engineering my year and in the classes ahead of me, but I didn't meet them and the black graduate students until much later. Though we all may not have been in the same classes, they were a tremendous help navigating the waters. My first quarter classes consisted of calculus and solid analytic geometry, introductory chemistry, freshman seminar on women's physiology, freshman English focused on African-American literature, and tennis.

I had always been very good in science. I was so looking forward to my chemistry class. I sat right up front of
the lecture hall so I could hear everything. I was eager.
Some of the folks at the dorm advised me that the professor I had was a bit of a jerk and was not interested in
students. But, I took the section anyway, it fit in well in
my schedule. The subject matter was fascinating. We
were learning about the Schrödinger equation. I was
"geeked." But when I would ask questions, Professor
Weinhardt would either ignore me, or act as though I
was impossibly dumb for not knowing the answer.
When a white boy down the row asked the exact same
questions, Weinhardt would say "Very good observation," and explain. I gradually stopped asking questions;
in fact I became too timid to ask anything. I drifted to
the back row of the lecture hall.

By winter quarter my first year, I had a new engineering advisor from the Chemical Engineering Department
whose specialty was biomedical engineering. He advised
me to be a chemical engineer major because I'd earn a
classical degree. Everyone would know that I completed
a rigorous program of study, something they wouldn't be
able to tell from an interdepartmental major. Anyway, he
said by the time I completed the course work he would

approve for a biomedical engineering interdisciplinary major, I would be only a few courses shy of being a chemical engineer. He was a good convincing advisor, and I settled into the chemical engineering track.

I also wanted to take some language courses. (My mother and father had always impressed upon me the importance of being well-rounded.) Still embarrassed about Russian, I took Swahili. I thought, Swahili: Where else would I learn it? My sister Ada Sue had taken Swahili in college. It was taught out of the Linguistics Department. The course was extraordinarily interesting. The linguistics professor approached teaching this language by discussing its historical basis and phonetic structure. For example, Swahili has no gender, but classifies object words according to the object's use and philosophical categorization. And even more importantly, the professor was interested in me.

My freshman year I also found African and modern dance classes, acted in the play *No Place to Be Somebody*, and was in the musical *Purlie*. I was starting to get into the flow of the school and social life.

Bell Labs actively wanted to increase the numbers of minority and women students engaged in engineering and the sciences. I had a National Achievement Scholarship, sponsored by Bell Labs. One of the additional benefits besides scholarship money was that the labs would employ its scholarship recipients during the summer. My experience at Bell Labs during my freshman summer gave me a respite from the struggle to be accepted by many in the science and engineering faculties at Stanford. That summer, I worked at Bell Laboratories in Naperville, Illinois. I learned the computer language PL/1 and refreshed the FORTRAN IV programming skills I learned in high school. I wrote computer programs that were used throughout the center. I read and documented existing programs, learned to troubleshoot some computer systems, and even occasionally was compelled to look through some BASIC and machine language code for bugs. I worked with two young white males, full time programmers who were impressed with all the work I did in such a short time.

Never a wallflower, second year I started asserting myself more. Sophomore year I took a political science class on Politics in Sub-Saharan Africa. It was taught by Professor David Abernathy, who was supposed to be one of the toughest political science professors at Stanford. The course was wonderful. Professor Abernathy demanded we read lots of books and analyze the information. He enjoyed my participation in his class, though I was not a political science or social science major.

I continued to dance. I was elected Black Student Union president. I kept up with Janet and my friends from my freshman dormitory, though I now lived in Laganita Court and the Black Theme House dormitory.

Over the four years my career at Stanford was marked by many extracurricular activities and student leadership. I designed and helped teach two classes at Stanford, one called Race and Politics in Education; the other, Race and Culture in the Caribbean. I became more and more interested in the history, politics, languages, and cultures of Africa. I continued to take Swahili classes just because I liked them. I took more political science and history courses on Africa and continued to take dance classes. I would even drive with Linda Jones and friends to Oakland to take African dance classes at Everybody's Creative Arts Center. All the while, I doggedly pursued my major in chemical engineering. I took classes of interest in the sciences and engineering, like Life Science in Space Exploration; Biomedical Instrumentation; and Biomedical Fluid

Mechanics (simultaneously with my first fluid mechanics course). All were graduate courses, but hey, this was information I wanted to learn. The professors seemed pleased that I found their courses of interest and gave me permission to attend. I rose to the occasion and did well in these graduate level classes.

Summers I worked at Bell Labs on printed wiring board materials and on nuclear magnetic resonance spectroscopy.

Fall quarter senior year while counting up course credits, I found I was just two required courses shy of fulfilling the requirements for a major in African and African-American Studies. I was on track for Chemical Engineering, as that's what I intended to do. But why had I taken so many of these political science, history, culture, and linguistic classes? I had just planned to be a science and engineering person. Certainly chemical engineering, which had the most course requirements of any Stanford major, kept me busy. So did my extracurricular activities and on again/off again social life.

I took the courses because they interested me and I realized even then, that the professors in those classes wanted me in their classes. They believed in me as a student, unlike the feeling I got in most of the engineering and science classes. I did not have to jump over hurdles each time I walked in the door just to prove I belonged there. The social sciences professors were interested in my ideas, insights, and comments. My intelligence was legitimate. Looking back, I realize that it was important for me as a student, to have professors who believed in me, teachers who felt that I could become one of their colleagues. I majored in African and African-American Studies because I was unconsciously balancing the poor reception I often received in the science and engineering departments with the embrace of political science.

I was probably a much better physical scientist than I was a social or political scientist, though my academic grades do not reflect it. But academically at Stanford, I could not afford to relinquish my heart, energy, and soul completely to the physical sciences because the majority of the professors pushed me away. Certainly I ran into some like the Physics Department chair who gave me an incredibly glowing recommendation for medical school and called me one of the most outstanding students he had met in his twenty-five years of teaching. He wondered why I did not major in physics. One chemistry professor called me to his office after one of my test scores was wildly variant (lower) from previous ones. We talked chemistry and he gave me an oral quiz. He suggested I become a chemistry major instead of engineering because they really needed bright students like me. I stuck with Chemical Engineering because I was determined to do biomedical engineering.

People ask me what was the most difficult thing about majoring in engineering: being a woman, black, or from public schools. I don't know. To finish engineering in four years, I had to adopt a "bunkered down" type of mentality. No matter what, I was going to complete engineering. I was determined to keep my sense of self, but it was bruised and bloodied. My self-confidence was intact and pulled me through; self-confidence built as a child and teenager, by falling down and getting up and knowing I was worthwhile, just because I was me.

I want to be clear that I believe my reception by the science and engineering faculty would have been the same if not worse at any prestigious predominantly white university in 1973. I consider it my good fortune to have been at Stanford where I had other outlets for my talents and where there were some professors who were not completely closed-minded.

The bad part of going off to school at sixteen was that I did not know that professors' sexism and racism could be so great as to be threatened by the presence of someone, a teenager, unlike them. I was unprepared for the assault on my capabilities. Clearly, I had had prior run-ins, epic disagreements with teachers and authority figures, black, white, male, and female. But, never had the people I looked up to and depended on for training doubted my intelligence and aptitude on sight. It was a harsh blow.

The good part of entering this environment at sixteen was that I was still just brazen, arrogant, and untamed enough that I could find ways around these obstacles. At sixteen and seventeen, I was still actively, aggressively exploring, pushing any limitation I came upon. And so though it hurt to have folks doubt me, I just didn't care enough about convention and adult standards of behavior to bow to their concepts of me and wishes that I would just disappear. I had no intention of doing so.

I had friends with whom I laughed and played. I had outlets for energy, enthusiasm, and frustration. I found small consistent means to maintain my sense-of-self and continue to build my self-confidence. I found ways to let the wind blow around me and then open my wings and soar on its currents.

WIND CURRENTS: THE WORLD AT LARGE, WHAT IT WAS TELLING ME, AND WHAT I HEARD ON THE WIND

Role Models and Images

Growing up, I pretended to be Honey West, a female private eye on television who had an ocelot. I liked that Honey West was in control, did not run to men or anyone else to save her. She saved all of them. Then there was the villainous Catwoman on *Batman*, played by Eartha Kitt. Catwoman did not always win, but I was captivated by her athleticism, sensuality, and daring. Oh yeah, I also liked Wonder Woman, one of the good guys, and Medusa, an evil woman in the comic books. I didn't like Sue Storm, The Invisible Lady with telekinetic powers, a member of the Fantastic Four, because she was always whining and crying up under her husband Reed Richards, Mr. Fantastic. I wanted to be like their nemesis and part of the cosmos like the Silver Surfer. When my brother, sister, and I played Flash Gordon, they always made me be Ming the Merciless. I developed an understanding of the villain. I tried to be cool and unemotional like Mr. Spock in *Star Trek*.

I had my hair cut into a short, natural hairstyle like Miriam Makeba in fourth grade. In high school I discovered Judith Jamison, the tall regal woman who was the star of the Alvin Ailey Dance Theater. That was a wonderful discovery, because already at 5' 7" as a sophomore in high school, I was tall for most women dancers.

Dr. Linus Pauling was great. He was a scientist who won a Nobel Prize in biochemistry and a Nobel Peace Prize for his work on trying to stop the atmospheric testing of nuclear weapons.

In college I studied Julius Nyerere, the president of the East African country of Tanzania, and how Nyerere worked to keep Tanzania politically non-aligned with either the United States or the Soviet Union. He wanted Tanzanians to determine their own path after colonialism. In medical school, I read of the handsome and charismatic Che Guevara, who was born into a world of privilege, a physician who chose to try to change the governance and policies of his country. He became a key political, revolutionary figure in Latin America. Che died violently at the age of thirty-nine. Isaac Asimov wrote with incredible clarity about worlds, peoples and technologies that existed only in his imagination. Arnold Schwarzenegger parlayed his muscled physique beyond a strong man statue into a new genre of action films. Shirley Chisholm in 1976 declared as a candidate for the Democratic Party nomination for President of the United States. Shirley Bassey sang the theme to the James Bond movie *Goldfinger* and every other song that had the good fortune to be chosen by her, with all the passion, understanding, and melody that is possible. Lola Falana danced. Gloria Steinem, while a journalist, posed as a Playboy Bunny and exposed the objectification of women, bringing attention to the fact that a new view of women was needed and feminism was real.

I never met most of these people, fictional or real, but each one was an image of what may be possible in this world. As public figures they were images that gave life to specific qualities and characteristics. I did not know what personal trials or tribulations they went through or how they managed to cope and excel in difficult times.

But the results were impressive. They stood as testimony to possibilities.

Each of these folks, the characters I mentioned, plus many others affected me, some more strongly than others. But they were not my role models, because I did not know them or interact with them day to day. I did not know what they did when things didn't go as planned, or if they brushed their teeth every night. How did they treat their husbands or wives? How did they treat their cats and people less fortunate than them? Did they work late into the night to finish a project? Did they sacrifice some of themselves for others or only do things for self-aggrandizement? Those types of skills and behaviors I learned from the people I lived with and interacted with every day: my mother and father, siblings, teachers, uncles and aunts, next-door neighbors, and friends. These people were my role models.

I learned grooming, how to care for my skin, and how to put on makeup from my mother, by watching her get dressed for work each day. By encouraging me to look things up in the dictionary, even when I was not sure how to spell the word, my mother taught me the importance of research and self-reliance. Seeing my mother go back to school to get her teaching degree, and later a

Master's degree, while raising three children was an enduring lesson in perseverance and lifelong learning. She always read about all kinds of subjects, read books, newspapers, magazines, and kept abreast of current events. I remember she would sew through the night if need be, to make sure we had new outfits for special occasions.

My father's support of my mother dispelled notions that a man must be in the foreground at all times. He worked while my mother finished college. I learned from my father that men should and can be responsible for fixing their own food and watching the children. He plaited my hair and got me ready for school. My father and his friends took me fishing and hunting. When I was seven, eight, nine years old, I learned how to paint, play the card game Bid Whist, and its art of verbal one-upmanship with these men who appreciated and bragged about my assertiveness, will, daring, and sharp wit.

When my uncle Louis spoke to me about Einstein's Theory of Relativity and the size and distance of stars, I learned that I should and could understand anything. When my aunt Melvyn unselfishly gave of her time on weekends, when she let me go to the dry cleaner with her and work, I learned how hard folks work daily and also how to diligently press clothes well, how to share with others, and the importance of family.

My siblings taught me how to study and make good grades in school, play chess, be cool, avoid parental wrath, and have fun. Ricky, Ada Sue, and I would stand up for one another, fall asleep on one another's laps, and forget the day's skirmishes. They would rock me to sleep when I was sick. Ada Sue held my hand as we crossed the streets and would let me go on dates with her. I already knew how to apply to college and get scholarships from watching her. Ricky took drafting classes which he did exceedingly well in and I learned what it was used for when he shared his experiences. My parents' tolerance of my science projects, that I always had to ask "why?" helped me incorporate tolerance of a little bit of chaos for a later good into my personality. These people, these role models, were the ones who made the biggest difference in my life.

WAFTS OF FORMALDEHYDE: MEDICAL SCHOOL

How I Really Learned to Study

It was not until medical school that I learned how to really study and be a full-time, focused student. Not that academics and chemical engineering at Stanford weren't challenging. I certainly did my full share of engineering problem sets, studied for tests, spent lots of time in the library researching term papers — in high school and definitely in college. I always turned in my homework, usually on time. It's just that medical school demanded that you study every day *after* being in class from nine to five! No matter how bright you were, how quick on the uptake, you still had to study.

There were volumes of information that had to be committed to memory. There was no grading on a curve, no "A" for effort or because you got fewer questions wrong than most other people. There was an absolute minimum amount of information you had to know, and know correctly, not "sorta" know. Think about it: Do you want your physician to "sorta" know where the major blood vessels in your arm are? Or "sorta" have an idea of how much medication to give in the middle of an emergency? Or only be able to prescribe one type of antibiotic because she hadn't bothered to learn about the others? Or better still, say "Wait, hold this bandage on your cut while I look up what vessel may be punctured. I'll be right back. Now, try not to bleed too fast."

Obvious to me now, but not when I arrived at Cornell University Medical College, CUMC, on 69th Street and York Avenue in New York City. My first priority in the selection of medical schools was to be in New York City, that's where I wanted to be. Cornell is one of the best medical schools in the country. It had great student housing and good financial aid. It was on the East Side of Manhattan, in one of the best areas of the city. I was very pleased when I arrived in New York City just a week out of sunny California. I'd spent the summer working as an engineer at IBM in San Jose, driving my new black Camaro and hanging out with a nutrition major from the University of California at Berkeley, a fellow Libran who called himself Mwalimu.

I took a week to drive the Camaro from California to leave it with my mother in Chicago. Though I had paid for it with money I made tutoring at Stanford, the provisions of my financial aid package to Cornell stipulated no cars. I understood. Why should they pay for you to spend $200 per month to park?

" 'Nuff said!"

Four years of growing up in California had molded me in certain ways, so, I stepped out of the cab in front of Cornell's Olin Hall with a nice, sunshine smile on my face. Californians, I found out later, were considered a bit "soft" by folks in New York — and we dressed differently. Remember this is 1977, and all the things we accept now were not the norm. In fact, the age of "profiling" in nightclubs — you know, folks standing around dressed fabulously, trying to look good — was moving into full swing. People described by the terms "yuppies" and "buppies" were entering the workforce.

Twenty years old, 5'9", 136 pounds, muscular, I entered Olin Hall dressed in tight faded blue jeans with holes in the knees and a few other places, a blue, faded denim work shirt tied around my midriff, sandals, hair in a hundred small plaits all over my head, two earrings in one ear and a feather in the other. I was armed with linear algebra, tons of differential and partial differential equations. I knew all about counter current flow and heat and mass transfer, and Reynold's numbers in fluid flow equations. I could speak Swahili and knew quite a bit about the politics of Sub-Saharan and Southern Africa. I knew a little more anatomy than the average dancer does. And I thought pre-med students had a tendency to be overly obsessive-compulsive and never really delved into the fundamentals of scientific theory and process.

I had an easy smile, good political acumen, social activism, initiative, and believed in myself. I could dance my fanny off. " 'Nuff said." Oh yeah, I played a diabolical hand of the card game Bid Whist and had bought a few new conservative outfits for fall.

I met my roommate, Joan Culpepper, a young woman who was a chemistry major from Smith College. We shared a bathroom between two adjoining rooms. Joan was cordial and friendly. I noticed that she already had some anatomy books out, and was reading through them. It was still two days before classes started, so I pegged Joan as a *real* "pre-med." (You see, I wasn't a real pre-med as I did not decide to apply to medical school until spring quarter my junior year in college. And I did not intend to practice medicine. In fact, one real pre-med friend at Stanford call me a "closet pre-med.") Still, Joan and I established an easy companionship that has lasted through to this day. We had many things in common I would later learn. I also found out that Joan always had "the scoop" about all things having to do with academics and medical school. From her, I learned that there were four black women and six black men in our class, thirty women, and 105 students total. Girlfriend had already scoped the books for class and knew upperclassmen and professors.

While Joan and I were talking, there was a knock on my door. Standing there was this 6'4" brother who could have easily, in all truthfulness, given Arnold Schwarzenegger a run for his money. His name was Blaine Morton, and he was a biochemistry major from the Massachusetts Institute of Technology. We all spoke "nice-nice" while establishing credentials. Blaine grew up in Long Island. Joan grew up in the Bronx and went to the Bronx High School of Science. I was from Chicago. Next thing I knew, Blaine looks me up and down and says something about Chicagoans and "caps" on my plethora of plaits! Oh, it's like that. Since this was clearly an intimidation tactic, rather than getting into a "signifying," or name-calling, contest I responded, "Blaine, don't make me kick your butt." Men are not used to women elevating the conversation to the physical so quickly, especially when they are big strapping bucks. Though I said it with a playful smile, Blaine didn't know if I was "kidding on the square." Joan just laughed as Blaine asked, "You gonna kick my butt?" My reply, "Right here, right now." Thereafter Joan, Blaine, and I became study partners. My introduction to members of the upperclass Cornell University Medical College community occurred later that evening at a social.

A get-together was held at Lasdon Apartments, to welcome the upperclassmen back and check out the first-year students. Still dressed in my California special outfit I walked with Joan to the high-rise building. There were about twenty people there, food, and a card game, Bid Whist. One of the guys suggested that the men play against the women. At some point Joan and I sat down as partners. For those of you who don't know, Bid Whist is a game with levels of strategies, just like everything in life. Bids are made based on how many books of cards you think you can win, as in bridge. If you make the number you bid or more, you receive the points. If you make fewer books, the entire bid is subtracted from your score. The first team to make seven points wins or the first team to go to minus seven, loses. There are of course many ways and strategies to win or force the other team to lose.

The other key component of Bid Whist is psychological intimidation, verbal one-upmanship or "talking trash." How colorfully you can verbally express how well you played, how poorly the others played, or cover your mistakes (*not* the position to be in)? Subtle movements, including not saying anything and just "taking names," that is, winning, also works as an intimidation technique. I could trash talk with the best of them. But I believe etiquette demands that when you're new and trying to make a good impression, you should be mannerly. So amidst all the conversation, Joan and I just "took names." We won and were polite. The fact I had gone to college in California implied to the folks from the East Coast that I might be a bit of a pushover, so they didn't know not to try certain stuff. After Joan and I had caused multiple male groupings to "rise and fly," one light-skinned brother from New York came in and asked, with a grin on his face, "How's it going? Are the girls losing?"

I tried y'all. I really did. I couldn't help it. I had been tired of being called a girl for a while. Black men would not tolerate being called anything with "boy" in it at all, so, why should I? I replied, "No, the women are winning and the boys are losing." My first day at CUMC.

That night I took my plaits down, washed my hair, and got my conservative clothes out for the first day of medical school orientation and class. Orientation consisted of, if I remember anything about it at all, someone telling us the schedule (many students already seemed to know it), information about physical exams and vaccinations that we would get, and syllabi for classes were distributed.

Gross Anatomy

Our first class was Gross Anatomy, at 9:00 Wednesday morning. In gross anatomy one learns about the muscles, internal organs, blood vessels, bones, and nerves. Basically, from my engineering point of view, these were the mechanical portions or the geography of the human body. I had seen Joan studying the dissection manual, a hint I ignored. I hadn't even bothered to buy my books yet. I sat in my seat shocked when after just 40 minutes of lecture hall discussion about the first dissection, and a small commentary about where the cadavers or human bodies we would dissect came from, we were given locker numbers, a group dissection number, told to change into our white coats, and promptly report to the lab. My internal dialogue with myself and the world began.

Wait, wait, wait! Don't you want to give us a chance to adjust? Explain what you mean by dissection, I've never cut a human cadaver. You mean the entire lab is filled with dead bodies? Who? Who goes first?

While I slowly walked into the lab, other *real* pre-med students rushed in excitedly. When I arrived at my table, I met my cadaver partners. They, being *real* pre-meds, were jockeying for position as to who would make the first incision. Not wanting to seem too out of it, the least I could do was stand close enough to see what they were doing, but no, I did not want to make the first incision or any other cut that day. Nor did I want to touch the cadaver. (Didn't we need to wave some special talisman over her or something? I found out it was a her, as the cadaver had one leg and one of my three lab partners quickly named her "Gams.")

Okay, everybody, just be cool. They haven't given us the special physician secrets. You know the *secrets*. The secrets that make it okay to cut someone open and look around inside. I am sure we need this information even if the body had been pickled in a large vat of formaldehyde for over a year, and the owner of it volunteered to donate it to medicine.

Oh, hell! Someone has already made a midline incision and is looking for the what muscle? Okay, the *rectus abdominus*. I asked aloud, "May I see your dissection book?" To myself, I said, "What's an atlas?" The dissection manual says, *"Identify the insertion of the rectus at the pubic symphysis."* The what? One of my other cadaver mates says to look for the aponeurosis. (Just keep looking at the dissection book.) It mentions that *caudally* . . . I'll flip a few pages ahead. I can't read this book. It looks like English, but I can't understand. Hell, I can't even say any of the words except for superior and inferior — but superior and inferior to what?

The formaldehyde smell is a bit overwhelming. ("No, that's okay, you go ahead and cut John, I'm happy looking.") It has *got* to be close to time to leave. How come no one else looks anxious?

Well, it *is* interesting that the muscles on the abdomen have a lengthwise structure that crisscrosses the abdomen almost like a girdle. Wow, look at that layer of yellow fat just beneath the skin. The muscle looks a bit like parboiled flank steak. Hmm, I didn't know human muscle looked so much like meat. Okay, Mae, you can make yourself touch it. You have gloves on after all, unlike those professors operating bare-handed. . . . There, I touched it. Feels a bit like stringy meat. Oh, everyone's starting to leave. I knew time should be up. Out of the lab coat. Careful don't let it touch any of my clothes. What's next?

Lunch at a New York deli. I'll wait 'til this evening. Sure am glad I like vegetables.

Two weeks later, I was better. In the gross anatomy lab, I could make incisions. Armed with a medical vocabulary and terminology workbook, I had come to understand the Latin roots of many medical words and how they described varying characteristics and locations. Oblique meant at an angle. If something was anterior, it was toward the front of the person; posterior, toward the person's back; cephalic, having to do with the head. Directions were always given based on the patient's right and left. Cool. Things were getting better. I had all my books, and I could even manage to eat lunch after gross anatomy lab. But, I still hadn't awakened and smelled the formaldehyde on the wind.

My lab partners and many of the other *real* pre-meds had this terribly annoying habit of quizzing each other or showing off by recounting the most minute details and obscure names of minor blood vessels and nerves, and where they started and ended. They worried about the names of normal and obscure variations to the anatomy. I wondered, "What's the big deal?" We can always look that up in a book. I'm trying to understand how the mechanical structure supports these activities. The other stuff is memorization. I figured the *real* pre-meds were just being obsessive-compulsive again. Yet, their behavior was so consistent; even Joan and Blaine did this. They would even go to the gross anatomy lab late at night to go over the dissection and the prosections of certain cadavers the professors made to illustrate specific anatomical points.

One day, wanting to assure myself that indeed I, the engineer, was right and the pre-meds were wrong, I spoke to

Professor Girkis. As he was demonstrating and naming what seemed to be a particularly obscure normal variation of the mesenteric arteries I asked, "We're not really expected to know this are we?" Dr. Girkis, who very much resembled the fat man from the movie *Casablanca* stopped and stared at me. I could see that any number of thoughts were fighting in his mind. Finally, he just answered "Yes." I can only imagine his incredulity.

Oops! I had ignored all the warning signs and explicit directions from the *real* pre-meds. My next weekend was determined in that moment. I sat down with my human body atlases, dissection manual, gross anatomy text books, and several pads of paper, and began to memorize all the names, points of insertion, bifurcations, origins, normal variants from the three weeks before that I had previously endeavored to "understand." What I now understood was that a different approach was needed. I read the text and dissections before class, and reread materials after class. I even joined Joan and Blaine in a few midnight forays to the gross anatomy lab to review the materials in-the-flesh, so to speak.

I called my sister Ada Sue, who was already in her fourth year of medical school, and asked her advice. She sent me all her neuroanatomy and extra gross anatomy books.

Joan had already recruited me into a biochemistry study group. She and I went over and over microanatomy (the geography and functioning of the body's cells) together. I was constantly amazed by Joan's organization. She had a place for everything. Joan rewrote her notes from class and then filed and classified them in subject-specific binders. In class Joan carried different color pens and markers that she used to emphasize the lecture information. Our first-year class also organized itself to take notes. Every lecture was taped and each student in the class took turns using these tapes to prepare lecture notes. These notes were then distributed to the entire class. Tests were pass/fail with an occasional high pass given out. I don't think there was a low fail.

At Stanford, I studied in the afternoon. My entire four years there, I had only pulled a couple of almost all-nighters, and they were only to complete typing papers. Occasionally I stayed up until 2 a.m. to complete problem sets. In medical school that all changed. Though I didn't do all-nighters, I often stayed up until 2 a.m. studying, especially during finals and for midterms. I would go to sleep at midnight and wake up at 4:30 a.m. to continue studying. On exam days, I always went to sleep by 1 a.m., even if I woke at 5 a.m. the next morning to do some "top off" studying. I believed it was better to be well rested so that my mind would have the best chance of remembering something I had read.

Never before had my class work been such an all encompassing focus of my life. I remember meeting people and seeing body parts, imagining where the splenic flexure of their colon was located. I visualized if the person I was talking to was accidentally impaled by a spear, with entry at the anterior right mid-line seventh intercostal space and exit at the posterior left tenth intercostal space what structures would be affected. That was like the questions asked in gross anatomy quizzes. "What structures, besides their entire lives?"

Still I was in New York City. The reason I had wanted to be there did not escape me. I found the Alvin Ailey Dance Studio on 58th Street and First Avenue. I spent what non-tuition, non-room money I had on modern dance classes, even if it meant my meals might be lacking. After my modern class, I always heard drums upstairs as I was preparing to leave the building. One day I ventured to the second floor and became totally enthralled with a Katherine Dunham technique dance class. Led by Joan Peters, the workout was hellacious, the choreography tough and rigorous, and the drums hypnotizing, as well as the drummers. (Damn, they looked good!) Dunham's technique, I believe, can best be described as African dance performed with a ballet technique. Katherine Dunham was one of the most exciting and original masters of dance in America. An anthropologist and dancer, she not only studied, but learned African dancing. She started the Katherine Dunham Troupe I believe in the 1940s. I definitely knew about her, but had never learned her technique. From then on, every Tuesday and Thursday when I had the money, I walked the ten blocks to class for the energy. And I would walk back no matter how cold or wet it was.

For recreation, Joan Culpepper and I joined pickup basketball games occasionally in the Olin Hall gym. The gym looked remarkably like a gladiator pit. It had tiled walls all around, with I am sure, concrete beneath the floor. The distance from the out-of-bounds line to the wall was not more than 3 feet on the sidelines and maybe 4 feet behind the baskets. The majority of the folks playing there were *real* pre-meds, with all the attendant baggage, some interns, and residents. Many were not particularly athletically talented. It was dangerous down there. Injuries were common. Anger flared. I heard all types of inventive curse words. Learn something new every day. Joan also played pool well so I would tag along and learn.

My eating habits also changed. When I arrived in NYC I did not drink sodas, did not eat candy, and no sweets unless I cooked them myself. I ate very few processed foods. By the time I graduated from medical school, I was routinely eating hot dogs with mystery onions off the vending carts along the streets. I went to Gil Scott-Heron concerts, Alvin Ailey and Dance Theater of Harlem performances, the New York City Ballet, and plays. Most Sundays I would wake up by 7 a.m., go to the deli, get a cup of coffee, and the *New York Times*. I'd enjoy the coffee and the *Times* before breaking out the books.

Later in the year Joan let me in on a secret. She was surprised I was so involved in student politics, was so knowledgeable about African-American history, and possibly seemed a bit radical. She told me she figured when they said I was from Stanford University I would be like, you know, a "California Girl." I would show up with a smiling surfer boy on my arm. Instead she and I wrote a script for a skit for the class Christmas show. The skit was based on one of our very serious, astute, quiet "Introduction to Clinical Medicine" professors becoming lost "uptown" (read Harlem) on a Saturday night. We recruited Blaine to be a co-hoodlum with Joan. A classmate Joel was the hapless professor, and I played the "Woman on the Corner" to help him spice up his life. I still do not believe I had the nerve to wear those hot pants and high-heel boots!

Extracurricular activities were an important part of school for me. My first year I had helped put together a pamphlet for high school students to prevent prescription drug abuse with Rupa Redding, a second-year student. We even went into one of the schools to teach students about this. After a summer of research and travel to Cuba with a medical student study group, I felt comfortable enough to become more active in student politics. As president of the Cornell chapter of the Student National Medical Association my second year, I helped coordinate a regional New York and New Jersey health and law fair with students at Columbia University's law school, and with medical students from New Jersey Medical and Dental, Einstein, New York University, Cornell, and Columbia. Third year I was elected president of the Cornell Student Executive Committee; my last year I was the student representative for Cornell to the Association of American Medical Colleges. This fulfilled my need for social activism, but also required a tremendous amount of energy. I committed political *faux pas* that caused me some grief with the administration, but, I also learned about the workings of medical schools and the politics in medicine.

I Can Learn New Tricks

By my second year, I adjusted to the rhythm of medical school. The first class was Microbiology and Microbiology Lab. This time I was ready. I knew how to pay attention to detail. I already had all of my books. I was ready. I was just not prepared for the fact that the blood for the experiment to understand how antibodies are produced as a result of typhoid vaccination would come from the students — us. They got me again!

After the lecture we went into the lab, took seats, and were told that the person next to us would be our lab partners. Cool. We had to take blood from one another, before giving each other injections of typhoid vaccine. Not so cool. Not only did I intensely dislike needles, but the guy sitting next to me, my new lab partner, looked like he couldn't tie his shoes on the first try. (No offense meant, but you notice these things when someone is about to impale you with a two-inch needle.) This was the first time the vast majority of us had ever tried to take blood, so the microbiology department generously supplied written instructions. Great! Let's just say my buddy was not successful on the first try. I have small veins. Experienced lab techs occasionally have problems with me. The professor eventually had to retrieve my blood. (Yes, I was able to get blood from my partner the first time.) Next came the vaccinations. He did a great job. Overall the lab was not too bad, until that evening when I felt hot, feverish, headachy, nauseated, and fatigued. These were "minor" side effects of the vaccination they wrote about that lasted only twenty-four hours. Oh yeah, the arm soreness may last up to two to three days.

The highlight of second year was Physical Diagnosis and getting medical instruments. Owning a stethoscope meant you really were becoming a doctor. Actually, you had to order your stuff before Physical Diagnosis started. That doctor stuff is expensive. My budget was limited so I didn't get the classic doctor bag. I didn't like it anyway. I got a stethoscope, syphgmonanometer (blood pressure cuff), opthalmoscope/otoscope combination, reflex hammer, tuning forks (What are they for?), flashlight, and white jacket. Now we're talking. We learned on one another how to listen to the heart, examine the eyes, assess the integrity of the spinal efferent and afferent peripheral nerves (nerves to and from the spinal cord) using the reflex hammer and tuning forks (so that's what they're for), estimate the size of the liver, and use new words like boborygmy for stomach growling.

I could do this. In fact I was pretty good with physical exams on my classmates.

I soon learned it was quite different asking a stranger to take off their clothes for me to examine them naked. Even though I helped the patient maintain their dignity with strategically placed small sheets, what about my embarrassment?

One of the greatest side-benefits of third year clinical rotations in medical training is realizing that you can stay up for thirty-six hours and still function mentally and physically. You learn not to resent circumstances because they happen to go awry or people when they get sick at times inconvenient to your schedule. Seemingly fighting it every step of the way, I learned to be precise and thorough so that my patients did not pay for my sloppiness with their lives or have sequela (bad outcomes), which I could have prevented with a bit more diligence.

A SOUTHERLY WIND
BLOWS . . . AFRICA

I spent the summer between my second year and third year of medical school in Kenya, a country in east Africa. Arriving there was really like reaching a destination I had dreamed about and moved toward all my life. As a child I cut my hair because of Miriam Makeba, I danced to Olatunji, I took African dance lessons in college, I majored in African Studies, and later I worked for the Peace Corps.

What do I remember most about my first trip to Africa? Several things. First, seeing the shore of North Africa as the plane crossed the Mediterranean. The

Mediterranean Sea sparkled blue and green. Then beneath us appeared the golden brown sands of the Sahara Desert. The Sahara Desert! Where camel caravans linked West African empires with Egypt. The Sahara Desert! Where many believe that thousands of years ago societies flourished in a savannah, before drought and time gradually turned it into an ocean of desolation. The Sahara! Home of the fabled city of knowledge, Timbuktu. Y'all, this was the desert where the pyramids and the pharaohs lived! A vastness that could hold the entire continental United States. I was over Africa! Africa existed. It was real and some of my ancestors had come from this place.

I had a grant from the International Travelers Association and student loan money to support myself while I was in Kenya. Besides going to game parks and partying, I held several jobs there. While in Kenya, I hung out with the folks at the African Medical Education and Research Foundation (AMREF), formerly the Flying Doctors. The Flying Doctors began as a group of physicians and other Western healthcare professionals who would travel into remote areas of Kenya and East Africa to provide health services, particularly surgery, to people who might otherwise go without. The Flying Doctors used airplanes because roads were often very difficult or perhaps nonexistent. Later they expanded their work to include more epidemiology, the study of people and the illnesses they have, and how those illnesses originate.

With AMREF, I helped perform a community health survey and diagnosis in the Embu district near Mt. Kenya. We walked from homestead to homestead in rural villages assessing the health of the people; measuring the height and weight of children; counting the number of people per household and vaccination status. I assisted with surgery performed using drip-ether anesthesia. I worked in a hospital and clinic in Voi District. There, in Voi I worked with a British surgeon and the head nurse mistook me for a member of his ethnic group, the Taita, rudely speaking Swahili to him instead of "our" Taita mother tongue. I was really fitting in! In Voi, I also saw a baby delivered for the first time. Amazing. It looked like it *hurt!* I saw a herd of zebra cross the road in our headlights as we traveled at night in a remote section of the Voi National Park.

When in Nairobi, Kenya's capital city, I roomed with Laura Tuthill, a fellow New York City graduate student in a Kenyan dentist's home. I met Laura as we went through immigration control at eleven o'clock at night.

Neither of us had a confirmed place to stay so we partnered on the spot and at one in the morning found a *cheap*, tacky hotel to stay in until we found permanent quarters. Laura was there for a summer internship with the United Nations Environmental Program office. The dentist we stayed with had been a student at the University of Maryland, where Laura's father was a professor who hosted him. So the dentist was returning the favor by hosting Laura. I stayed with the dentist and his family when I was not traveling outside of Nairobi with AMREF.

Through the dentist, I was introduced to private clinical health care in Kenya. I also met members of the Kenyan Hindi community. Though the dentist was Luo, one of the major Kenyan ethnic groups, and of African ancestry, many of the other dentists were from India. I helped them by editing transcriptions of guest lectures of the Kenya Dental Association meetings.

Nairobi in 1979 was an attractive city with bougainvillea vines, magenta, fuchsia, pink, white, orange, and red, spilling over the walls and center dividers of main thoroughfares. Large marketplaces sprawled. Odors of piquant spices, fish, meat, and fruits in all states of freshness wafted in the air. Open stalls were hung with brightly colored fabric and baskets for sale. The stalls displayed household products and second-hand electronics. When it rained, puddles formed in the mud. Extreme poverty was apparent, right next door to opulent wealth. Old, colonial-style houses were scattered in high-income neighborhoods. Downtown was filled with shops, restaurants, and office buildings. Mostly two- or three-story rectangular, stucco buildings with flat walls lined the streets. Occasionally, high-rise buildings up to twenty stories, like the circular building destroyed when the U.S. Embassy was bombed in 1998, bespoke modernization. There were large modern conference centers and movie theaters. I saw *Moonraker* in one. James Bond was a hit in Kenya.

I rode the crowded city buses around Nairobi and learned how to muscle my way inside. (Not too much trouble for a Chicagoan and current New Yorker used to riding the "el" train and subways.) Matatus, however, were a different story. These privately owned vans and small buses regularly picked up people and carried them to their destinations. The doors hung off. The crowds inside put Tokyo subway cars to shame. New York cabbies would not stand a chance driving against them. My heart was not up to the challenge. I avoided them.

In Nairobi it was great to be able to go into any hair salon and get my hair done. One day, one shop, and its people stand out in my mind. When the proprietress asked the woman cornrowing my hair how much I owed, the hairdresser did her calculations out loud in Swahili. She did not know I could understand. She said she would have to charge me a bit more because I had a "kichwa kubwa" and "nyele nyingi" — a big head and a lot of hair. When I laughed, everyone in the shop looked around and laughed, too. It was the camaraderie and belonging that felt so wonderful.

I was ready to be in Africa. I was well prepared. I knew Swahili. I had studied the politics of the region. I had studied the history and culture before, throughout, and after colonialism. I knew the geography and some of the issues of development. I completed a four-week course in parasitology with emphasis on diseases of the tropics just prior to coming. But, I really wasn't exactly ready for Kawangware, where I helped with some community medicine projects while in Nairobi. Kawangware was unexpected.

Kawangware, a huge slum, sat on a crowded expanse of land on the outskirts of Nairobi. It gathered in people who left the villages in rural areas for the perceived advantages of the cities. Many of them could not afford Nairobi and Nairobi did not welcome them. So people ended up on this bare expanse of red dirt, where ditches along the side of the road served as open sewers. The ditches overflowed with too much rain. Poorly constructed mud homes with zinc-pan roofs overheated and leaked. Lean-to structures built of discarded, but recycled pieces of lumber kept the rain out, sometimes, and the goats and chickens in or out depending on one's preference. All around, I could see the despair in people's faces, but I could feel the hope and determination in their hearts as they swept porches and carried water on their heads. Illness lurked around corners in darkened lean-to shacks, but the possibilities for tomorrow swirled the red dirt in the streets, as children pushed each other in small carts.

I remember the arguments and conversations I had with Kenyans about African Americans. To make a long story short, many Kenyans thought the black folks in the Tarzan movies were African Americans playing African Americans. So Tarzan movies managed to misrepresent black folk on both sides of the Atlantic in one fell swoop.

I left Kenya after eight weeks to travel to North

Africa and Egypt, Greece, and Israel. I spent two weeks traveling before returning to the United States and the dreaded medical school third-year clinical rotations.

I stepped off the plane in Cairo, planning to stretch my funds by traveling around on my own. I had already contacted a student hostel, I had a guidebook, and I knew most of the places I wanted to go. But I decided to sign up for formal tours after being leered at by a soldier at the airport, though I wore a very modest, long skirt and quarter-length sleeve blouse. I looked around the airport and I realized most the signs were in Arabic. Not only couldn't I read them I couldn't even remember the letters. Egypt would be difficult to travel around safely and cheaply on my own, so I met and traveled with a young New Zealand couple. We were put together by a travel service that I signed on with at the Cairo airport.

I saw the pyramids of Giza and the bazaars of Cairo. I saw, as well, the layers of religion and signs of the occupying forces that this pivotal locale of human civilization has experienced. The early history of Christianity in Cairo represented by the Coptic Church was fascinating. Islamic history came afterwards. At the Luxor Temple, on the Nile, I was struck by the immense scale to which everything was built during the time of the pharoahs and the vibrancy of the colors after all the thousands of years. The tombs in the Valley of the Kings and Queens were cool and provided relief from the noon sun that burned my skin in thirty minutes. I even got to Tutankhamun's — King Tut's — tomb.

I traveled through Athens airport, but I was forced to skip seeing Greece. I had spent all my money except for about seventy dollars to take the formal tours in Egypt. So I boarded the plane for Israel, hoping to charge a tour package with room included on the credit card my mother had given me. On the Olympic Airway flight I sat next to an American Jewish woman who was returning to her home in Quiryat Tivon, after vacationing in the United States for a few weeks. Incredibly, she invited me to stay with her and travel around Israel the next week as she still had some time off.

I stayed with her in a kibbutz, met a former operative of the Israeli Secret Service Mossad, visited the Sea of Galilee, and the hillside where Jesus Christ is said to have given the Sermon on the Mount. We sat talking in 100 degree weather after my companions convinced me to get into a hot sulfur spring to cool off. We were on a hillside overlooking a flat expanse of land. The former Mossad operative pointed out that I was looking at the

Golan Heights and Syria, just 10 kilometers away. He explained that Israel was a thin strip of land that was difficult to protect. I heard his recollection of the Seven Day War.

In Jerusalem, I went to the Dome of the Rock, which I learned was the most holy place in Islam after Mecca. It was said to be the site from which Muhammad ascended to heaven. That very same place is also said to be the place where Abraham was to have sacrificed his son.

My friend dropped me off near the Wailing Wall where she would meet me later. She did not feel comfortable in the Arab Quarters of Old Jerusalem. I traveled Old Jerusalem on foot. I followed the Via Dolorosa, the path Christ was supposed to have taken as he carried the cross on the way to his crucifixion. One of the stops on the walk was at an old church that had an area open below its cellar. Cobblestone streets from the days of Christ were visible and cisterns built by the Romans still stored rain water. The journey ended at the Church of the Holy Sepulcher, which some say is the site of Christ's tomb.

From all these places in Egypt and Israel, all the people, the ideas, one on top of the other, Judaism, Christianity, Islam, Palestine, Israel, Romans, Nubians, and pharaohs, I began to understand the complexity of the politics — and I also saw faith. I felt the wind gathering energy and I understood that until we humans fully acknowledge how intertwined we are with one another, there will be endless suffering.

THE WINDS INTENSIFY

When you graduate from medical school you just have a degree. You do not have a license to practice medicine. To get a license, in most states you need to complete at least an internship; then you can work and also pay back all the loans you accumulate while in college and medical school. After internships, physicians complete residency programs to specialize in things like pediatrics, psychiatry, etc. During internship and residency training, new doctors are paid very little to work in hospitals about eighty to ninety hours per week. While doing this they gain experience in patient care under the supervision of more experienced doctors. It's not involuntary servitude, but it feels like it sometimes. I went to medical school because I wanted to do biomedical engineering research, I never intended to practice medicine. So I had never intended to pursue a residency program. While at Cornell, my travels to Cuba, Kenya, and a Cambodian refugee camp in Thailand taught me that I was fascinated by medicine in developing countries — primary care, basic medicine. I learned so much about the world and myself. I knew that I wanted to have a longer experience in those environments.

Therefore, I decided to apply for what was called a one-year rotating internship with nothing — graduate school or medical residency — nothing scheduled afterward. Having nothing scheduled would force me to actually plan something overseas. I figured I could come back and go to graduate school in engineering later.

Back up, rethink this. At least that's what the deans at Cornell said. I was summoned by two of them. They implored me to apply for a residency program. After all, they told me, I was graduating from one of the best medical schools in the country. Cornell alumni were expected not only to be board certified in surgery, pediatrics and obstetrics and gynecology, internal medicine, or other specialties, but to do more in-depth fellowships afterward. You know, like pulmonology or prenatal care. Here I was just doing an internship, a flexible internship at that.

I explained my plan to go to work in the developing world, then go on to graduate school in engineering, to pursue biomedical engineering research. One dean said I was making a terrible mistake. He explained that in ten years I would be far behind my fellow classmates and feel less accomplished than them.

I did feel scared, but I decided this time not to get the classical degree and go the regular route as I had at Stanford. Just like Joan always said, it seemed I was wasting a perfectly good clinical medicine slot and doing something somewhat strange and California with it.

I spent the following year in Los Angeles at the Los Angeles County-University of Southern California Medical Center — LAC/USC Med Center, the largest county hospital, training more in pediatrics, infectious diseases, surgery, oncology (cancer medicine), obstetrics and gynecology, and emergency room work. That year served to solidify my practical knowledge in general practice medicine. At LA County Hospital you certainly had a lot of different cases and patients to work with. During that year I also investigated ways to travel overseas and work in a developing country.

I applied to many organizations and noted on my applications that I would go as a physician or an engineer, whatever they needed. After speaking with a Peace Corps recruiter about a position in Papua, New Guinea, setting up a computerized database on the nutritional status of the islanders, I was told of an opening not for a volunteer, but a paid staff job with responsibilities for the health of volunteers. I applied for and was selected for this position in West Africa.

As Area Peace Corps Medical Officer for Sierra Leone and Liberia, at twenty-six years of age I was responsible for the health of all the U.S. Peace Corps volunteers, staff members, and embassy personnel of Sierra Leone and the Peace Corps volunteers in Liberia. I managed a medical office, a laboratory, pharmacy, and volunteer health training as well as acted as the primary care doctor. I encountered diseases I had only read about in tropical medicine textbooks. I worked with Sierra Leonean physicians and nurses trained in the best schools in England and Germany, but who were at times forced to work with little or no equipment, medication, or supplies. I cared for a patient in Freetown with acute encephalitis when there was no electricity. I assisted in the appendectomy of my best friend's son; I oversaw the autopsy of a person who may have died of Lassa Fever, a hemorrhagic virus and the one infectious disease that truly frightened me when I read about it in medical school.

On call twenty-four hours a day, seven days a week for two-and-a-half years, in a place so unforgiving of mistakes, I gained flexibility, knowledge, interpersonal relationships skills, and an appreciation of the challenges life poses to so many people on this planet.

The harmattan, the winds blowing off the Sahara desert in December, blew cool, dry air and brought haze to the skies of West Africa. In spring they stopped, the sky cleared, and light rains fell. And in the same way the dilemma I faced — how to balance and integrate my love of advanced science and technologies with my love for travel, other countries, and other cultures was solved. As the misconceptions of what life is like and what the challenges and opportunities in poor countries are, cleared, I understood. What we decide to do with our talents is up to each one of us and is based on our view of life and our desires. My talents — physical sciences and social sciences — are as applicable and important for the development of inexpensive but effective systems to bring clean drinking water to millions of people in rural villages as they are to help a person suffering from renal disease in the most prestigious hospital in New York City.

WIND CURRENTS:
REALITY LEADS FANTASY

"*The phase distortion is clearing. Transport window will open in two minutes,*" Lieutenant Palmer reported. She watched Commander Riker, Lieutenant Commander LaForge, and Lieutenant Worf as they waited for Lieutenant Riker to report to the transporter room. Lieutenant Palmer, a tall female human from Earth with a very close cropped hairstyle was not normally on transporter room duty. In fact, she was new to the crew of the Star Ship *Enterprise*. Her last mission had been on the Space Shuttle *Endeavour* over 200 years before. Wait a minute . . . in addition to the transporter problem that created two Rikers, there's a little time distortion issue here.

My appearance on the *Star Trek: The Next Generation* episode "Second Chances" in 1993 was the completion of a circle that began in 1966 the first time I saw *Star Trek* on television. At LeVar Burton's invitation, I became the only *Enterprise* crew member to have actually gone into space. I felt quite honored to be on the set, and in a way become a small part of the *Star Trek* family.

When *Star Trek* premiered, I was only ten years old, but I already knew that I would travel in space. I had a set of encyclopedias that gave the step by step details on how a human would arrive on the surface of the moon. I had latched onto the study of how the universe began, how stars were formed, how life began and evolved on Earth, and the future colonization of other planets as a lifelong interest.

Much to adults' dismay, I had defiantly pronounced that NASA and anyone else who tried to explain as reasonable the idea that women were not suited to be astronauts were nonsensical. There was no explanation except that the folks controlling the programs stupidly just did not want women to participate. I stand by that to this day.

As I said, I had already decided that I would go into

space. The fact that all the U.S. astronauts then were white men just made it a little more difficult, a challenge. Though the Russians had sent up a woman cosmonaut in 1964, not many people around me seemed to share my conviction that I would travel in space, which made things a bit complicated. My parents supported all my science projects and whims, but I still don't know if they were true believers or shared my enthusiasm for space-flight.

Then came *Star Trek,* with Lieutenant Uhura, Mr. Spock, and Lieutenant Sulu. Wow! Somewhere, some-one else believed that other kinds of people would popu-late spaceships from Earth. Humans of all gender and ethnicity would be in space. Here was affirmation. *Star Trek* immediately captured my imagination and respect. Amid the scares of nuclear proliferation and annihila-tion, moral and ethical conflicts concerning criminal jus-tice, nationalism in colonies, the second and third waves of racial riots in the United States, and the promise and uncertainty of physical science advances, *Star Trek* pre-sented a hopeful view of humanity and the future.

Star Trek dealt with issues of our time, then and now, in the safety and glaring spotlight of the future and sci-ence fiction. Topics like the bitter animosity between two creatures based on what they considered incredible differences: the characters were literally half black and white on different sides of their bodies. Differences that in their society heralded inferiority bigotry and which warranted oppression. *Star Trek* episodes considered when and why violence is ever acceptable. What is the difference between good and evil when both seek conquest of the other? Why shouldn't humans be used for experiments and gambling as we would use other animals today? There was pseudo-scientific talk and mysteries in the middle of societal issues. How do we define life? Must intelligent life look like us? Must it be based on carbon? Can computers supplant humans in command structures and decision making? Just what is warp factor one and how does anti-matter drive an engine?

Amidst all these positive affirmations, incongruous human foibles still flourished. Every time "Bones," the physician, wanted to insult Mr. Spock, he would say something disparaging about Spock's Vulcan blood and mixed human and Vulcan parentage. Ditto if Captain Kirk wanted to insult Spock. An episode that absolutely outraged me was when it was revealed that women could not be star ship captains. (This was in 1966, pre-Captain Janeway on *Star Trek: Voyager*). This woman, who was more qualified than Kirk, switched places with him through an ingenious mind-switching device just so that she could have the command of a star ship. She became overbearing and made poor, emotional decisions. And Kirk, inside the woman's body, was the calm, reasonable person he never was in masculine garb. You know, I just had a problem with that whole scenario.

My overall favorite characters were Mr. Spock and Lt. Uhura. Mr. Spock was "The Man." I thought he was particularly cool, not only because he was brilliant, but also because of his insight into humans and their behavior. He provided that reflecting board to make sure we paid attention. His "lack of emotions" and logic were an interesting approach to dealing with life.

Lt. Uhura. What can I say? I always wanted to see her on screen. I believe she was the first woman to appear regularly on television in a technical role. She was intelligent, skilled, gorgeous, cool, and looked a bit like me and the women around me. She had a wonderful soothing voice and manner. I was disappointed that she did not get more airtime.

I met Nichelle Nichols, the actress who played Lt. Uhura, after I was an astronaut. In fact, I was at Kennedy Space Center (KSC) participating in the Terminal

Countdown Demonstration Test (TCDT) for STS-26, the first launch after the *Challenger* accident when I heard her on the radio. Ms. Nichols was being interviewed on a morning talk show to publicize a *Star Trek* convention taking place in Orlando, Florida, over the Labor Day weekend. Now, not being a "real" Trekkie — you know those people who wear *Star Trek* costumes, buy the paraphernalia and schematics of the star ships, and know all the titles of the episodes (either because I didn't have enough money or already had a life) — I had never been to a convention. But I thought it would be cool to meet Lt. Uhura, since in some ways, she was instrumental in my being at KSC.

Nichelle Nichols and her company, Women in Motion, were pivotal in the recruitment of the first women and minority astronauts in 1976–77. When NASA decided to admit women to the astronaut program and actively sought non-white male participation, they ran into a problem. Over the years of being rejected and seeing only one face of the right stuff, many other faces having the right stuff — women and men of color — didn't believe NASA was serious. So for the class of astronauts that would crew the new reusable vehicle, the space shuttle, NASA received very few applications from those previously spurned groups. NASA looked for a way to convince folks they were serious. NASA and Nichelle found each other. Nichelle, with no personal compensation, underwent aspects of astronaut training, made public service announcements and traveled across the country to draw the attention of individuals with qualifications to become astronauts, but who did not respond to NASA alone. I personally remember the public service announcements and the effort. But alas, I was still in college then, and though precocious, too young and without a college degree. NASA would have to wait.

Back to 1988. I recruited the Kennedy Space Center Life Sciences physician, Dr. Irene Long, who was also a big science fiction and *Star Trek* fan, to go with me. Here's the situation. We arrive at the convention. I was a bit shy, but I thought what the heck, I'll just go up to the convention producers and tell them who I am and that I want to meet Ms. Nichols. Right? Exactly who was I? I was dressed casually and looked younger than my thirty-one years. I was an African-American woman at a Trekkie convention trying to see one of the legends of *Star Trek*. Would they believe I was an astronaut as I smiled and said it? Well, it was worth the try.

Surprise, surprise. After I found the fellow they told me was in charge, I announced, *"My name is Dr. Mae Jemison. I am an astronaut working at Kennedy Space Center and I am here to meet Nichelle Nichols. I think she might want to meet me also."* Guess what? He said to follow him and he would ask her. We walked to her hotel room. He told us to wait outside the door. I didn't know if Nichelle even knew my name. Next thing I knew, I heard her saying *"You have Mae Jemison waiting outside? Bring her in immediately."* I was embraced in a warm hug. And we have been close friends since.

Due to her mother's illness Nichelle was unable to come to the launch of my spaceflight, but I spoke with her the night before. And I began my shifts on orbit with a variation of Lt. Uhura's trademark call *"Huntsville,* Endeavour. *All hailing frequencies are open."* The circle was complete.

HARNESSING EXPLOSIVE WINDS

Endeavour

"*M ae, come up to the flight deck,*" I heard over my headset as I worked to complete the stowage of the orange launch and entry suits. Still in my lightweight thermal underwear from launch, I pushed off and floated through the opening from the middeck to the flight deck. Hoot, the commander of STS-47 Spacelab J, the fiftieth flight of the space shuttle, pointed out the window. "*Chicago is coming up.*"

I peered out.

The first thing I saw from space was my hometown. Chicago looked just like it did on the map. The grayish color of the concrete, barren land, and buildings of the metropolitan areas outlined the city against the green of the surrounding farmland. I thought about being a little girl down there and smiled. I watched Chicago leisurely pass from sight. My hometown passed from horizon to horizon in less than five minutes.

I thanked Hoot for calling me and returned to the middeck to complete the stowage timeline. I removed the launch chairs, finished the suit storage, pulled down some cue cards, and put up others. Now alone, 160 nautical miles above Earth's surface, we, the seven-member crew of the orbiter *Endeavour*, on its second flight, were transforming it from a rocket into a space laboratory.

During the mission, I was scheduled on the "Blue" shift with Drs. Jan Davis and Jay Apt. The Blue shift worked during the hours which basically corresponded to nighttime in the United States; the "Red" shift corresponded to daytime. Jay, who has his Ph.D. in Physics from Harvard, was on his second mission, and was the MS-2, Mission Specialist 2. His job was to attend to those things that kept the shuttle *Endeavour* itself operating smoothly during our shift. Jan, who entered the astronaut program with me in August 1987 was part of the payload crew and has a Ph.D. in Mechanical Engineering from the University of Huntsville. She was married to another member of our crew, Air Force Colonel Mark Lee. Jan, Mark, and I had trained for over two years, much of the time in Japan, to learn about the experiments we'd be conducting on this flight. Japan is where we met and trained with Dr. Mohri Mamoru, a Ph.D. in Fluid Physics, who rounded out the payload crew. Mamoru was a payload specialist on his first spaceflight and was the first Japanese national to fly aboard the space shuttle.

Mark and Mamoru were on the Red shift along with our commander, Navy Captain Robert "Hoot" Gibson, and the pilot, Air Force Captain Curt Brown. Hoot and Curt worked like Jay to keep the shuttle running smoothly during the Red shift.

The job of the payload crew, Jan, Mamoru, Mark, and I, was to do all the "real work." The experiments that the shuttle carried into orbit took advantage of the microgravity environment. This is an environment where objects have very little weight. Gravity is still present, but its effects are counteracted. We worked in the "shirt-sleeve" conditions of the spacelab, a 23-foot long pressurized structure built by the European Space Agency

(ESA) that fit in the payload bay of the shuttle. The spacelab is a reusable laboratory that can be installed in any of the various space shuttle orbiters: the *Discovery*, the *Atlantis*, the *Columbia*, or the *Endeavour*. (By the way, the airplane-looking part is called the "orbiter" because it is the only piece of the whole launch stack that actually orbits Earth.) Our mission, called Spacelab J, carried over forty-four different experiments ranging from material sciences and development of new semi-conductor materials (that's the stuff computer chips are made of) to biology and how frog embryos develop in weightlessness. The experiments were designed by investigators from across Japan and the United States. Some of the investigators or scientists worked for NASA or NASDA (the Japanese Space Agency). Others were researchers from universities and private industry.

We had seven scheduled days of experiments. Additional days could be added if the shuttle supplies lasted. Our orbital inclination was such that we crossed the equator at a 57° angle and so were able to see northern Japan, in fact all of the earth between the latitudes 57° north and 57° south of the equator. On liftoff, the shuttle's main engines combined with the primary lifting capabilities of the solid rocket boosters had generated

7,781,400 pounds of thrust accelerating the *Endeavour* from 0 miles per hour to over 17,000 miles per hour. In the roughly eight minutes it took us to ascend to space, we not only reached 17,500 miles per hour, but also traveled over the Atlantic where the solid rocket boosters dropped into the ocean to be retrieved for reuse. As we climbed to an altitude of over 160 nautical miles, we flew over Africa to the Indian Ocean where we attained orbit, the main engines shut down, and the external tank, separated from the orbiter. The external tank, which had supplied all the fuel for the shuttle's main engine on ascent, tumbled into the atmosphere and burned up. Meanwhile, the orbiter and its crew began the process of establishing our home in space.

Once we were in space, Hoot fired the Orbital Maneuvering System (OMS) engines, to "circularize" our orbit from an elliptical shape so that our lowest point (perigee) and highest point (apogee) were basically the same altitude. Hoot, Curt, and Jay opened the payload bay doors, and used the Reaction Control System (RCS) jets, to change *Endeavour*'s attitude so that its tail pointed to Earth while its nose pointed toward the darkness of space. This positioning of the shuttle to Earth's surface gave us the best radio communication signals with the ground and allowed us to radiate away all the heat that the equipment on board would generate to the coldness of space. The orbiter's radiators or cooling system are part of the payload bay doors.

Meanwhile Jan, Mark, Mamoru, and I worked to prepare the rest of the shuttle for our week of experiments. It all seemed so simple. The panels filled with switches and circuit breakers were so easily understood now. All the procedures flowed smoothly. All so easy and uncomplicated from what I would have imagined when I first stepped inside of a shuttle mock-up in August 1987 after reporting to the Johnson Space Center, Houston, Texas, an astronaut candidate, or ASCAN as they called us.

This Is Houston . . .

On a cold, rainy January evening in 1987, I grabbed my mail as I ran up the stairs to the second-floor landing of my apartment building in west Los Angeles. I was a little tired after working all day as a doctor at the Cigna Health Plans west L.A. facility on Sepulveda Boulevard. I took an aerobics class at Voight Fitness in west Hollywood afterwards, so I was in sweaty tights, leotards, Reeboks, and a sweatshirt. Now I was home and could shower, eat, and rest.

My cat Sneeze, whom I got as a tiny kitten in Sierra Leone, jumped up and greeted me at the door with lots of love and affection. His green eyes and loving caresses on my leg alerted me. I wondered what he was up to and looked around my one-bedroom apartment for tattletale signs of misbehavior. Nothing wrong that I could find easily, so I plopped on the couch. Sneeze climbed on my lap and meowed loudly to give me a proper welcome home.

I shuffled through the mail. There it was. I thought I had seen it. An envelope from NASA. I opened it and found forms to be completed for background checks and security clearances for my application to the astronaut program. Wow! At least NASA was still interested. It had been a year since I had last seen this same set of forms. But before I had a chance to fill them out and return them, the *Challenger* had blown up on January 28, 1986. And all the world had just stopped to stare and try to understand.

NASA postponed the astronaut selection process for 1986 and informed the applicants that they would keep their applications on file. The selection office would let us know when NASA would start looking for new astronauts again.

The requests for updates arrived in fall of 1986. So tonight I completed the security clearance forms, and sent them in quickly. I waited to see what would happen.

A few weeks later I received a telephone call asking me if I was available to come to Johnson Space Center (JSC) in Houston, the following week for interviews. NASA interviewed a total of about 100 people out of approximately 2,000 qualified applicants. Fifteen of us would ultimately be selected.

In a week? Well, yeah sure. But, how was I going to get a week off from patient care on such short notice without everyone knowing? I didn't want folks to know I was applying to be an astronaut. I mean, who would think you were for real or sane? So, I went to Beverly, the office manager, and told her not to tell anyone. She arranged my time off. I told one other person. Sylvia Tanner. Well, the secret didn't last. Of course, when I got back from Houston everyone knew where I had been.

Believe it or not, I was as excited or more so when called for the astronaut interview than when I was selected. Why? Because, I had looked good on paper! My college and medical school transcripts that I fretted over were fine. The recommendations, my job experience, even the two-and-a-half years I spent in West Africa as a physician, which I thought would seem strange, must have been good. Wow, I would get to go to Johnson Space Center!

The next day I dashed to the UCLA bookstore at lunch time and bought books on the history of space exploration to study before I got to JSC. I called to arrange my flights to Houston. I tried to control my excitement. I only told my family. I got a couple of suits to wear in Houston for the interviews. Darn, I had just cut my hair into this slightly hip-hop Afro style. Just a week ago I was wearing it parted down the middle, and up in two "schoolmarm-ish" braids. Now how am I going to look conservative enough for the people at JSC? Well, I gotta go with what I've got now. I just won't spike and tease out the bangs in front.

. . . Is There a Problem?

So what do you do over a week of astronaut interviews? Medical exams of every form. Through the exams, the flight surgeons were attempting to establish that the applicants were physiologically normal. After all, astronauts are placed in abnormal, hazardous environments and it's most helpful to begin with as normal a physiology as possible. They looked for all types of chronic illness or physical and physiologic anomalies. (Perhaps some of my patients got together and called up to give them suggestions for tests to run.) There were eye exams with dilated pupils by ophthalmologists, sigmoidoscopy, sinus X rays, blood tests, muscle strength tests, hearing tests, psychological tests, and a full physical exam. A personal favorite was an isolation/claustrophobia test where I was asked to sit inside a three-foot-diameter balloon with air blowing in it for 30 minutes. I was to write my impressions of the experience afterwards as well as write up any modifications I would make to the sphere as a rescue device. I got in and started to hum and sing to myself, then fell asleep. The operator said I was the first one he had seen do that.

During my physical, the flight surgeon told me he heard a heart murmur. I told him I knew all about it and had first learned of it in medical school. The doctor at Cornell said it was a functional flow murmur, a fancy medical way of saying, that because of the shape of my chest wall and the way my heart was positioned, one could hear the blood flowing through it. None of my medical school professors had ever been concerned about it, but the flight surgeons were.

After the physical I just sat and smiled to myself, thinking it was a good try. I was sad that a nonthreatening murmur was going to disqualify me as an astronaut, but that was life. The flight surgeon said he would refer me to a cardiologist for an echocardiogram to see if there was any abnormality with my heart valves. Great! I wasn't out of the game yet. Once the echocardiogram was done and read, I was examined. The cardiologist agreed — it was just a "flow murmur."

I left Houston still in the game. Weeks went by. Some of my friends called me to tell me that they had been interviewed by the FBI. One joked, "I told them, yeah she can take and follow orders, but she is not going to walk off a cliff without a damn good explanation." I spoke with the FBI, told them all my secrets. I waited. It was almost like the trip to Houston had never happened. Things settled down. I continued to attend business and engineering classes at UCLA at night and worked at Cigna Health Plans. By this time I had been transferred to the main Cigna facility closer to downtown Los Angeles.

One afternoon in June, I was seeing a patient for lower back pain. As is my custom, I spoke to him about his symptoms, and stepped out of the room to record some notes in the chart and wait for him to undress. As soon as I walked into my office, my desk phone rang. I picked it up.

"Dr. Jemison, may I help you?"

"Is this Dr. Mae Jemison?"

"Yes it is."

"This is George Abbey at NASA and we wanted to know if you still wanted to be an astronaut."

"Yes. Absolutely!"

"Well, we would like you to come on board. We will release a formal press notice announcing everyone selected tomorrow at noon. So please don't tell anyone until after that."

"Great. Great. This is great. What do I do?" Huge grin.

"Someone from the astronaut selection office will get in touch with you and you will get more information. Thanks, Mae. Glad you're joining us."

"Thank you."

I grinned. I sat. I grinned some more. I said to myself,

"Now you've done it." I can't tell anyone. No one? What about my parents? Surely them. Not my sister, she talks too much. God, this is cool. Wow!

Okay. It's been ten minutes, get back to your patient. Don't be all "cheesed up" and everything. Composure. You're a professional. I settled my face into my "doctor look" and I walked back into the examining room. The patient told me about back problems and I began to do a complete physical exam. As I started to look at his pupils he asked what that had to do with his back. Snapped back to reality, I mumbled something lame like "just a thorough neurological check." I completed the exam and the rest of the day without a hitch.

I went directly to my favorite cardiofunk aerobics class. I was in high gear. In fact, I felt so great I stayed for a second advanced regular aerobics class. By the time I arrived back to my apartment I was still pumped. I called my parents, told them, and made them swear not to tell anyone else. (That's how secrecy is lost.) I told Sneeze we were moving to Houston. He was completely cool with it.

I decided the fitting thing to do was to stay up until midnight and watch reruns of *Star Trek*. Afterward, I finally went to sleep.

The next morning I woke up with barely time to shower, dress, and look kempt. I jumped in my car and drove the forty-five minutes to work. As I was walking out of an examining room that morning my nurse Juan Torres came up to me and said, "You didn't tell us did you, Dr. J?"

"Didn't tell you what?"

"That you got accepted to the astronaut program."

"How do you know?"

"Because, there have been ten phone calls from news stations trying to reach you. The messages are on your desk."

My life had changed. Those messages were a sign that sometimes you can't go back.

Roger that . . . Everything is Looking Good

When we first arrived in Houston, the task was to get everyone in my astronaut class to a common baseline level of information about human spaceflight. We had test pilots, a meteorologist, astrophysicist, mechanical engineer, a medical doctor (me), and a NASA flight controller in our class. We did parachute and survival training, not for use with the space shuttle, but for contingencies with the T-38 supersonic aircraft astronauts fly in.

That's right, I said supersonic aircraft. Two-seaters. I had flown on the Concorde with a patient in tow and an IV drip running when I was a doctor in West Africa. But now we're talking oxygen masks, helmets, call signs, gauges, and ejection seats. As a Mission Specialist I was not expected nor trained to fly the planes on my own, but rather to be a useful crew member in the back seat: to handle the radios, fly straight and level, follow headings and flight course to be able to control the plane once off the ground, and plan the flight.

We learned about spacecraft and orbital dynamics. Spacecraft are very different from airplanes and how one flies airplanes. We learned of the human body's response to weightlessness and the hazards of spaceflight. We learned about the history of human spaceflight, what happened to cause the *Challenger* accident, the innards of the space shuttle, NASA sites, aerospace contractors, and research. Planetology, geology, meteorology.

And we learned about one another.

Just before the de-orbit burn that would bring the *Endeavour* and our crew back to Earth, I perched quietly, looking out of the windows on the flight deck. Strange, but I always knew I'd be here.

Looking down and all around me, seeing the earth, the moon, and the stars, I felt just like I belonged right here, and in fact, any place in the entire universe. And I had known since I was seven years old that the universe was a very big place. Floating up in there in the shuttle, I tried to imagine what it would be like to never travel into space again, to remain forever on Earth. And that felt just fine, which I would never have guessed.

And then I imagined that I was traveling around a star 10,000 light years away and would never return to Earth. And that felt just fine, as well. In fact, I felt so calm that I realized I would feel comfortable anywhere in the universe — because I belonged to and was a part of it, as much as any star, planet, asteroid, comet, or nebula. Didn't my body and my mind contain the same atoms and energy as do the stars?

WHERE THE WIND GOES

The air stirred by the heat of the engines as the space shuttle roared into the sky not only shook the viewing stands six miles away with a chest rattling rumble, but also my future.

I was not only the first African-American woman in space, but the first woman of color in the world to go into space. The trip brought fame and fanfare: 1993 *People* magazine's "Fifty Most Beautiful People in the World"; honors and awards such as induction into the National Women's Hall of Fame and the Johnson Publishing Trail Blazer Award; letters from people around the world; requests to appear in commercials and to commentate on TV news programs, and even to host television programs. But most significantly my role in the spaceflight provided me a stronger, more visible platform from which to discuss the importance of individuals taking responsibility not only for themselves, but also for how they treat others and this planet.

I resigned from NASA in 1993 and started a technology consulting company to pursue my ideas on integrating social issues into technology design. The Earth We Share (TEWS) international science camps, and programs arose from my ideas about the most important reasons for science education — critical thinking and problem solving skills. I began teaching Environmental Studies at Dartmouth College in Hanover, New Hampshire. As a professor I am challenged by students to continue my personal and professional growth and I challenge them to understand the myriad possibilities in the world. I give talks. I design projects with engineers, physicians, anthropologists, and entertainers to try to ensure that all people know that they have a place in this world. Each one of us has the right and the responsibility to live up to our individual potential and ambitions.

So many things have happened since I left NASA. Many good, and unfortunately a few tragic and sad. I have traveled widely and taken up new causes.

Every now and then, while walking outside in my neighborhood in Houston, or in Tunisia, or the Arctic, I feel a slight breeze on my cheek. I look around me. I look up at the sky. Maybe I will see the moon, a star, or the sun. I study my surroundings. Perhaps it's a beautiful flower that captures my eye. A bird. A cat slipping home after a late night out.

I look around me. I may see derelict buildings or a beautiful palace. I have visited the pyramids again. I saw the Nile from space. Perhaps I see the John Hancock Building towering above me on a Chicago morning. I may be distracted by the pain, the misery, or the immensity of problems facing billions of people worldwide. Yet beauty is always there. There is hope. And the breeze tickles my face and I know I have unraveled some of its secret. Ah, but there stirs another leaf . . . and I know for the rest of my life I will continue to new places the wind goes.